ROADS AND TRACKS
FOR HISTORIANS

Sychnant Pass
(old route to Holyhead)

ROADS AND TRACKS
FOR HISTORIANS

Paul Hindle

Phillimore

2001

Published by
PHILLIMORE & CO. LTD.
Shopwyke Manor Barn, Chichester, West Sussex

ISBN 1 86077 182 3

Printed and bound in Great Britain by
BUTLER AND TANNER LTD.
London and Frome

In memory of Dr. Bill Rollinson
Lake District historical geographer, 1937-2000
– a great colleague and friend

CONTENTS

ACKNOWLEDGEMENTS

My greatest debt is to Gustav Dobrzynski who has produced many of the specially drawn maps for this volume; his work has both artistry and clarity. Historic map extracts were provided by Harry Margary of Lympne Castle, Kent, Rex Russell of Barton on Humber, and Tony Phillips of Keele University. Other items came from the map library of the School of Geography in the University of Manchester and from the author's own collection.

The photographs were all taken by the author, with the sole exception of Fig. 113, which is used by permission of Peter Thornton from his book *Lakeland from the Air* (1985). The transport geographer Dr. Richard Knowles was kind enough to read through Chapter 9 to check on matters more current than historical.

Any errors of fact, undue emphasis, or omission are the sole responsibility of the author.

INTRODUCTION

The importance of roads in the study of history has long been understated or even ignored. Roads are a vital component of most historic events, such as war, trade, urban growth, industrialisation and migration. Throughout history roads have been fundamental in allowing and promoting economic growth, and they have always provided the backbone of the transportation system, even after the advent of canals, railways and air travel.

Four very different examples will illustrate how important roads have been in Britain's economic development. First, in the prehistoric period, tracks allowed stone axes to be traded throughout the country. Second, the Romans imposed their roads in order to defend this part of their northern frontier. Third, medieval towns were established principally in order to trade, and most of the goods were carried by road. Fourth, the increasingly complex agricultural and industrial systems of early modern Britain required the efficient movement by road of goods, people and mail.

Roads developed alongside other features in the economy and landscape in a classic 'chicken and egg' relationship. They are important in that they have allowed virtually every other feature of the landscape to develop, and have themselves developed because of those features. Individual elements of the landscape, such as castles, towns, villages, estates, mines, mills, woods and fields all required roads in order to be created and to function effectively. And roads are an important historical and landscape feature in their own right.

The levels of population and economic activity, often influenced by personal and political decisions, determine the number and relative importance of roads. The route each road takes is then controlled by the landscape through which it has to pass, and by the level of technology available (i.e. the means of transport and, if the road was being built, road-building techniques). All these factors are significant whether we are looking at a Roman road or a modern motorway.

An important distinction has to be made between those roads which were deliberately planned and built, and those which came into being simply through the continual passage of people, vehicles and animals. The latter essentially made and maintained themselves, and (apart from the Roman roads) were the norm until the creation of the turnpikes. Moreover, roads underwent a continual process of change in response to the changing needs for them; for example, the Roman road network did not remain the same throughout the four hundred years of Roman rule.

It seems rather strange, therefore, that there are so few books about roads which go beyond simple (and often drab) descriptions of routes and dates; much of the Roman road literature falls into this category. Other books are dusty texts concentrating on the legal aspects of roads, whilst yet others deal with related topics such as travel, travellers, conveyances, conditions on the roads and road-builders.

Many economic history books talk glibly about the growth of trade, towns and industry, but totally ignore the routes along which the goods were carried. Indeed, the study of the history of roads in the context of economic growth has been slight. In terms of particular types of roads, those built by the Romans have received much attention, but there is much less written about such an obvious topic as drove roads. Canals and railways, on the other hand, have received exhaustive treatment, with rather more books dealing with their relationship to the economy and the industrial revolution, and with their impact on the landscape.

There are numerous county-level historical studies which largely ignore the development of their road systems. On the other hand, in some areas, such as Derbyshire, Lancashire, the Lake District, Wessex, the Yorkshire Dales, and Dartmoor, the roads have received varying levels of study, but there are still few integrated road histories for most parts of Britain. In an age of increasing leisure and travel it is all the more surprising that this should be so. Many visitors drive around from one tourist honey-pot to the next, admiring this, photographing that, but ignore the fascinating history of the very routes along which they travel.

One reason for this neglect is certainly that roads are such a commonplace feature of the landscape that they are taken for granted. Anyone travelling from one place to another in most parts of Britain will find a road or track, and the only problems will be whether to travel by foot, bicycle, bus or car, how long it will take and how much it will cost. In less developed or more mountainous parts of the world, the importance of roads (especially when they are poor, or do not exist at all) is better realised.

This book has three aims: first, to recount the history of the roads of Britain; second, to place that story in the contexts of economic development and landscape change; and third, to give guidelines for further research.

The book cannot hope to give complete coverage of all the roads and tracks of Britain. It is simply impossible to mention, let alone detail, more than a few of the roads of each type in a single volume. The examples are intended to outline the general principles, so that roads elsewhere (in *your* part of the country) can be compared with them, and put into a wider context. Equally, some important exceptions to general rules are mentioned, but you should always be prepared for individual examples not to follow the general pattern. This book will have been successful if you want to ask questions about the origins of roads in areas which you know or visit; go and search out the library evidence, and then get out into the countryside to follow particular roads.

The approach adopted is basically chronological, starting with the ancient tracks, and working through to the motorways. But it will soon become very obvious that most roads and tracks do not belong solely to one particular period. For example, many of the earliest tracks were subsequently used by the Romans, by medieval traders, later by drovers, and some have now been made into long-distance footpaths. Yet there are a few single-period roads, for example Roman roads which have not been used since the departure of the Romans, 18th-century military roads soon abandoned, or mine tracks leading to derelict mines; however, these are in the minority.

A handful of road types do not fit easily into this chronology, and these 'unusual' roads are dealt with in a separate chapter. The main value of a chronological approach is that it allows a view of both when particular types of road or track were created or first came into use, and how the road network grew and changed. It is important to remember that roads have to be studied as a system rather than as individual routes, for they rarely functioned as the latter.

This is not a guide book, and thus no map references are given; however, there is always enough detail given for individual examples to enable a route to be followed on the appropriate 1:50,000 or 1:25,000 Ordnance Survey maps. Numerous illustrations are provided, including both old and specially drawn maps, and photographs. In any case, roads are such a commonplace feature, that most people are familiar with most types of road; though whether they have understood what they are seeing, in particular when, how and why those roads came into existence is another matter. This book hopes to provide some enlightenment.

Anyone with an enquiring mind, and a bit of time, inclination and energy can help to increase the sum total of knowledge and understanding of the development of British roads and tracks. The best possible result of the publication of this book would be the writing of new studies, whether at local, county or regional level. They might deal only with one particular historical period, or with a particular type of road; or they might attempt a complete integrated road/economic/landscape history of an area. Much remains to be done.

SOURCES

The available sources for each type of road are mentioned throughout the book, but it is useful to give a brief outline here. They fall into three categories: documents, maps and evidence in the field.

Documents

A vast range of documents may mention roads or travel. Anglo-Saxon charters and medieval grants often mention roads as boundaries. Later itineraries and diaries show that someone actually travelled along a certain route. Industrial records may reveal the routes used to move goods. Parliamentary journals and papers give details of the passage of turnpike and enclosure bills. Topographies and descriptions may detail what roads were in use, and newspapers or letters may provide comment on proposals for new roads or roads in bad condition. Parish records, particularly the vestry minutes and highway surveyors' accounts, can be useful, as the parish was responsible for local road maintenance from 1555. There are also the minutes of highway boards (usually found under Quarter Sessions proceedings), and then those of the local and county councils.

The records of the turnpike trusts themselves, plus various government returns, are of obvious interest, as are the records of tramway and bus companies. Old photographs may show roads as they were as far back as the mid-19th century, and sketches and drawings go back much further. There is an endless variety of documents, and it is impossible to give a complete list. Virtually any class of document may reveal some information about roads (Stephens, 1981). A day or two spent in the local history library or record office may be very rewarding.

Maps

Maps provide an extremely valuable but surprisingly rather under-used source (Hindle, 1998b). The early county maps of Saxton and Speed do not show roads, but later ones do, notably from the 17th century, often based on Ogilby's road strip maps of 1675, and later the lists of roads in Cary's *New Itinerary* of 1798. Maps show roads as one feature among many in the landscape; in particular, the large-scale county maps of the late 18th century are an extremely valuable source, showing the newly-created turnpikes, as well as much of the finer detail of the road network. During the 19th century the more detailed products of the Ordnance Survey progressively replaced these maps.

In addition, there are many examples of specific road maps (i.e.: those which show little else). The first are Ogilby's strip maps, but others include the parliamentary deposited plans and other plans of proposed road changes. Virtually any type of map may depict roads: estate and tithe maps, enclosure maps and even the plans for new canals and railways may provide useful information. To help with fieldwork an old OS 6-inch or 25-inch map (preferably First Edition: surveyed 1841-88) is ideal. Vertical aerial photographs can also be useful; there are various local and national collections, and they have been used to help trace Roman roads in particular.

Field evidence

Detailed library work is a necessary preliminary, but at the end of the day it is always more exciting to get out into the countryside, whether by car or on foot. This may enable you to see why the Roman or turnpike surveyors chose a particular route, why a packhorse track or drove road went a particular way, or why a route has shifted its course over the years. What may be unclear from the map or the documentary record may be stunningly obvious on the ground.

Most old routes are still rights of way, and there are normally few problems of access. Unfortunately, there are quite a few landowners who regard their land as sacrosanct, even where it is crossed by a right of way; do not be put off by signs saying 'Private Land' in such a situation. It may be worthwhile consulting the definitive footpath map for an area before setting out, not only to see where you may walk legally, but also to spot some of the many long-disused roads which still survive as footpaths. The Countryside and Rights of Way Act 2000 will soon give a much wider 'freedom to roam' over large areas of mountain, heath, down and common land in England and Wales (see The Ramblers' Association web site).

Many old routes have left physical or buried remains in the landscape which can be observed or which may have to be excavated. Roads which have been deliberately engineered, such as Roman roads or turnpikes, may have a structure which can be identified by sectioning. But those roads which came about through the continued passage of people and animals may have left nothing more than surface features such as ruts or holloways, or may have disappeared entirely from the landscape; even Roman roads can disappear after two thousand years. Another problem is that because so many roads have a long history, older surfaces have been buried beneath later ones and may have been destroyed, or made inaccessible. However, modern roads often deviate from earlier routes, and in such places the older routes may still survive, little used but still intact.

There is, however, one serious problem in field observation, namely the great difficulty of dating a road in the way that one might date a house or a castle; only rarely does field or archaeological evidence provide a date. But the simple existence of a road in the landscape at a specific date is not particularly important, as it may not have been in use. It is better (and often easier) to obtain a combination of documentary and map evidence for both the existence and the actual use of a road.

Two footnotes have to be added. First, the old (pre-1974) counties are generally used in the text, as their boundaries were the ones in use for most of the periods covered, and are still normally used in historical literature. Second, references to more detailed reading are given throughout the text; the books or articles referred to are listed in the Bibliography.

Chapter One

EARLY TRACKS

PREHISTORIC TRACKS came into use as part of the complex history of different peoples, cultures and invasions from the Stone Age through to the Iron Age. Wandering animals and the earliest peoples must have created some tracks, but it was the arrival of the Neolithic (New Stone Age) farmers around 4000 BC which seems to have led to a sudden increase in the number of settlements, and no doubt of tracks too. Their economy was based on farming rather than on hunting and gathering, they cleared large areas of trees for fields, and they began to trade, often over great distances.

Recent archaeological discoveries have shown that, from this date, populations generally increased fairly steadily, and the need for tracks must have grown accordingly. Indeed, this growth was helped by the climate which was warmer than today from the fourth to the second millennia BC. Stone and Bronze Age populations were clearly much larger and more sophisticated than was once thought, and trade continued to grow during this period; the items traded included agricultural goods, salt and tools. Stone axes from the central Lake District were produced from 3000 to 1500 BC – they appear to have been traded by both sea and land, and have been found throughout Britain. No doubt someone has already identified a Neolithic 'axe road', but it would be very difficult to prove such an association.

The fact that these early Britons built barrows, stone circles and then henges is a measure of the complexity of their social and economic systems. The evidence is thick on the ground in such classic places as the Wiltshire Downs, but even remote wet and windy Cumbria has twelve large stone circles dating from before 1500 BC. In order to build such essentially 'useless' monuments a society requires organisation, leadership, settled conditions, a surplus of food and the ability to trade. There clearly must have been an evolving network of tracks to serve the growing economic needs of those times. Life was becoming settled instead of nomadic, and definite tracks were needed to link one place to the next, as well as to more distant places.

Finally, in the years before the Roman occupation, the British began to build hillforts; evidently the need for defence had become important, perhaps because of invasions of new settlers from the continent of Europe. Each hillfort served a large local population, which had helped (or been forced) to build it, and which might benefit from its protection in times of unrest. Settlements were often grouped around these hillforts and were linked to each other socially, economically and politically, as well as by physical tracks.

Beyond these local links, obvious lines of communication across the country would probably have run along the treeless ridgeways, leading so often from one hillfort to the next. This explains the concentration on ridgeways as the typical prehistoric routes, which is so apparent in the literature. By the time the Romans arrived, the ancient British tribes (by now in the Iron Age) were farming most of

1 *The West Kennett stone avenue links the ancient ritual centre of Avebury with the Ridgeway; it was probably constructed in about 2000 BC, and is one of the oldest datable roads in Britain.*

lowland Britain, as well as many upland areas; the distribution of their hillforts is a clear indication of the density and extent of their settlement. Trade had become very important, and the items involved included metals such as iron, tin, copper and gold, as well as food, tools and even wine.

But finding good evidence of the existence and use of tracks in this period before written history is immensely difficult. Some tracks have been identified on the ground, whilst others have been seen as crop marks on aerial photographs. However, it is impossible to date such tracks. Few, if any, were deliberately constructed, for like medieval roads after them, most simply came into being through the continuing passage of people and animals. Despite this difficulty, topographic literature is full of unsubstantiated references to roads having prehistoric origins; no doubt many do have such a long history, but proving it is a different matter.

Nevertheless, it is very likely that many routes in use today have prehistoric origins, and this leads on to the notion that

> the idea of continuity is central to a consideration of the evolution of roads. Once a 'way' became established, its general line would be used over the centuries, though its *actual* course came to vary according to the type of traffic it carried and to locally changing patterns of land occupation and ownership. (Colyer, 1984.)

This continuity makes proving the date of origin of a track even more difficult. Virtually the only prehistoric tracks which can now be even vaguely identified as such are those which have survived because they have continued to be used, improved or altered in later times. Some Roman improvements fossilised prehistoric routes, whereas the more recent cattle drovers tended only to destroy any evidence which still remained.

We are never likely to be able to reconstruct accurately the network of prehistoric local tracks, simply because they are unlikely to have survived intact, and even if they have, they cannot be dated. Many have probably been in use for many thousands of years, and the

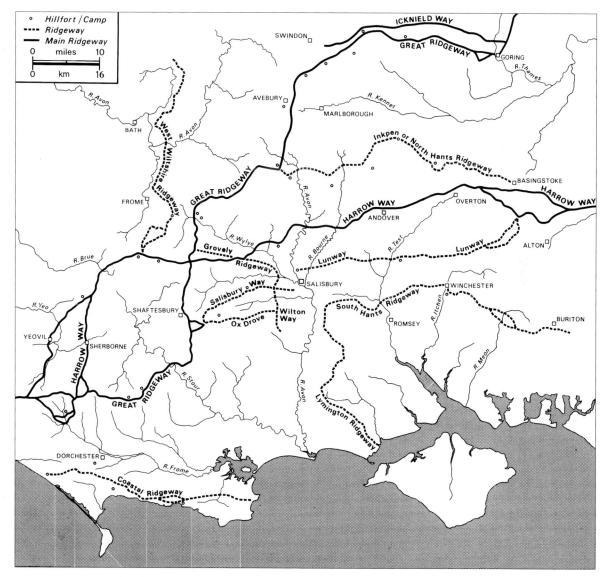

2 *The Wessex Ridgeways. Many routes have been identified, often with little evidence for their prehistoric use. (After Timperley and Brill, 1983)*

20th-century footpath sign, or layer of tarmac may well represent only the most recent act in a very long series of changes.

This lack of historical evidence has led to much speculation; perhaps the most famous is the work of Alfred Watkins (1925), who sought to find natural 'ley lines' running through the landscape, giving a network of 'old straight tracks'. Any objective study of his curious ideas reveals random alignments and

associations, and his notions of a race of Stone Age road builders are best forgotten. The very idea that Stone Age men needed sight-lines, markers and cairns to find their way about is something of an insult to them; they clearly knew their surroundings intimately. More recently, others have tried to see more complex geometric patterns and even reflections of the zodiac in the landscape. It is tempting to suggest that if you believe in any of these notions,

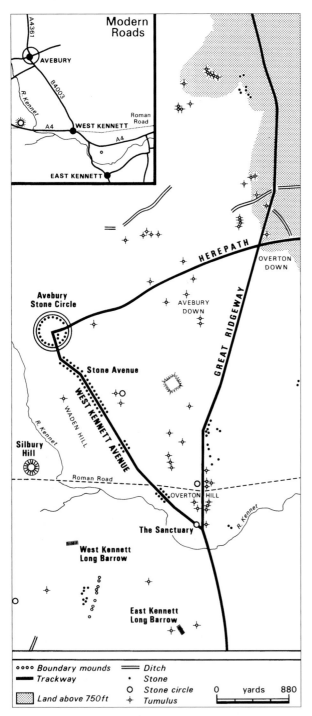

3 *Ancient routes near Avebury. The modern Ridgeway footpath represents what was formerly a much wider route. The West Kennett Avenue, a Roman road and a Saxon herepath (army road) can also be seen.*

then you may well be able to see the patterns – essentially 'they have to be believed to be seen', and that is no basis for serious scientific enquiry.

Occasionally archaeological evidence of ancient tracks does survive and the best examples have been found in the Somerset Levels. Here Neolithic farmers had to build tracks across the marshy ground in order to reach the 'islands' in the marsh; the Sweet Track from the Polden Hills to Westhay is the most famous. Their construction indicates a great pressure on resources at this early period. Over forty tracks have now been found, the earliest, dating from about 3000 BC, consists simply of bundles of twigs held in place by pegs; but by about 2000 BC there is evidence of more elaborate construction using planks or split logs (Wright, 1988).

In the monumental landscapes of Wiltshire, a deliberate creation of stone-lined avenues did take place in about 2000 BC. From Avebury, the mile-long West Kennett Avenue led to a stone circle called 'The Sanctuary', which was very close to the Great Ridgeway (Figs. 1 and 3), whilst Beckhampton Avenue led off south-westwards towards a group of round barrows. The precise purpose of such avenues is not known, though their function was probably ceremonial rather than connected with trade. However, on other parts of the Downs (and elsewhere) the physical remains of a few local prehistoric tracks have been observed, linking farms to their fields (Taylor, 1979). A complex pattern of such tracks clearly existed before the Romans arrived, but their history is often difficult to unravel, simply because the routes in use were constantly changing, and many have continued to be used, on and off, ever since.

The traditional first step in tracing prehistoric tracks in an area is to plot all the known sites that prehistoric man occupied, whether farms, monuments or forts; any surviving tracks linking such sites may well have prehistoric origins. However, this is a difficult process because our knowledge of the distribution of prehistoric sites, and of farms in particular, is very meagre.

As already noted, the best known prehistoric tracks of Britain are the ridgeways, but Taylor (1979) has thrown a good deal of doubt on their origins and importance. They achieved their status largely because they were seen to be closely related to the places where the most obvious evidence of prehistoric peoples was to be found, notably on the Wessex downlands. There is certainly no doubt that the ridges themselves are liberally scattered with prehistoric remains. It was originally thought that the valleys were then still filled with impenetrable forests, and that people would have had to use the ridgeways in order to get about. This is perhaps best summed up in Timperley and Brill's *Ancient Trackways of Wessex*, first published in 1965, which gives an exhaustive (and exhausting) description of every possible ridge route in Wessex. In 32 chapters, they name over a dozen ridgeways plus their numerous branches, as well as various other ways and tracks (Fig. 2).

The argument now levelled against the ridgeways being important prehistoric routes is that the distribution of prehistoric sites and finds as known today does not reveal a particular clustering along many of these ridges. It appears that earlier researchers may have fallen into the trap of basing their ideas on very limited data. The first prehistoric sites to be noted were the obvious remains on the ridges and downlands, but more recent work has shown that most prehistoric settlements were actually in the valleys, on what must have been better land even then.

In Northamptonshire, Taylor demonstrates that the so-called 'Jurassic Way', which was first proposed in 1940, running along the Jurassic limestone ridge, simply does not act as a route connecting the numerous prehistoric sites which were known forty years later. He makes a very convincing case for this route

being a 20th-century invention. Taylor goes on to show that even the Icknield Way, which is undoubtedly a prehistoric route, is also not particularly well related to the known prehistoric sites, and his conclusion is that none of the ridgeways was particularly important as a prehistoric route.

It can, however, be argued that this evidence is largely irrelevant. If a suggested prehistoric route is not closely related to the archaeological sites, then perhaps this may be simply because the two are largely independent of each other. The factors which must have influenced the location of farms, forts or burial sites are not necessarily the same as those which controlled the direction of travel and thus the creation of routes. The ancient Britons surely preferred to live where there was good quality well-watered land. But their criteria for choosing a route might have been very different: a route had to go in the appropriate direction, and it ought to be easy and safe to traverse. In these respects the ridgeways may or may not have been suitable.

Thus the fact that known prehistoric sites do not cluster along a route is not a particularly good argument that the route was not then in use; more detailed local examination is needed in each particular case. A much better argument against the use of the ridgeways is their lack of water for animals. Many of these old routes were certainly in use before the Romans arrived, but precisely when they came into use, and how important they actually were, will probably remain an insoluble mystery. Overall, the balance of the argument is probably in favour of their prehistoric origins, and they may be the first 'highways' in more ways than one.

Several of the ridgeways are described here; the best examples are those which traverse the downlands of southern England. But it is important to realise that originally they must have looked very different from the way they appear today. They were certainly less pronounced and much wider, as they were only rarely constrained by other features in the land-scape. By contrast, modern tracks are usually fenced or hedged in, and even today's tracks across open hillsides are probably much narrower and more obvious than their prehistoric counterparts. Further, it has long been suggested that most had 'summer ways' which ran along lower routes, used in dry weather when there was no water on the top of the ridge. Whether these summer ways are prehistoric in origin is impossible to determine, they are just as likely to date from medieval and later times when these routes were used for the droving of large numbers of cattle.

This suggestion of duplicated ways may, however, be based on a limited study of the modern landscape. It is much more likely that, until the downs were enclosed in the last 200 years, all the ridge routes were simply much broader than at present as there were no walls, fences or hedges to constrict the routes. Thus they were probably not the simple single or duplicated tracks and lanes which appear on maps today, but were much broader lines of travel, perhaps a mile or two wide, along which each traveller, trader or drover chose the best route available.

THE GREAT RIDGEWAY AND THE ICKNIELD WAY

This immense route stretches across England from the south coast near Axminster to the Wash (Wright, 1988). Perhaps its most famous section is that crossing the Marlborough Downs east of Avebury (Fig. 3). One guidebook describes this section as:

> a distinct and unmistakable track, seldom hin-dered by overgrowth or obstruction, swinging along mile after mile between widely spaced fences or hedges. (Jennett, 1976.)

Overton Hill now marks the start of a modern long-distance footpath along or close to this ancient route (Curtis, 1999). Until this new footpath was created in 1973, many parts of the old track were derelict, or used only as

farm tracks. Thus after a long period of neglect, the Ridgeway has re-emerged in its new guise as a long-distance footpath.

For the first few miles north of Overton Hill, the route crosses what is a landscape with many visible ancient features – a glance at the map or at the landscape shows Silbury Hill and the Avebury stone circle and avenue to the west. In addition there are numerous tumuli, ditches, standing stones, circles, earthworks, field systems and barrows; amidst all of this (and largely ignoring it all) the present Great Ridgeway path climbs straight up on to the downs towards Hackpen Hill. There are indications of other old roads here: a Roman road and the Wiltshire Herepath (a Saxon 'army road') both soon cross the Ridgeway. The fact that the herepath heads straight for Avebury suggests that it too had prehistoric origins.

After 5½ miles (9 km) the route passes close to Barbury Castle, the first of many hillforts along the way. The present ridgeway path does not actually pass through any of these forts, but as we have already seen, the prehistoric route was probably much wider than today's enclosed track, and thus the old route was well able to serve the forts if needed. The forts were deliberately situated on the top of the scarp, whilst the present ridgeway is rarely on the ridge, keeping just below the skyline (Fig. 4). The idea that the ancient Britons wanted to keep out of sight is pure conjecture; the present confined route between the hedges was probably only fixed within the last 200 years, when the farmers, enclosing their fields, left a narrow track for the drovers who still passed by (Fig. 5).

Just before Barbury Castle, the line of the Great Ridgeway as shown on OS maps descends from the ridge for several miles, whilst the modern Ridgeway Path goes straight through the castle, keeping to the ridge. At one point the two routes are almost 4 miles (6 km) apart; this modern bifurcation no doubt mirrors the

4 *The Ridgeway path running westwards from the hillfort at Uffington; the modern enclosed path is some distance from the edge of the downs, the scarp overlooking the Vale of White Horse is half a mile to the right.*

situation in prehistoric times. Twelve miles (20 km) further on, in the Vale of White Horse below Uffington Castle, the 20th-century metalled equivalent of this old route is the B4507, but it runs along the foot of the scarp. Both roads were clearly still in use when Rocque drew his county map in 1761 (Fig. 6).

Going eastwards, the name Icknield Way first appears on maps as a road below the main route of the Great Ridgeway to the north of Lambourn Downs. However, north-east of the Thames crossing at Goring gap, this name is adopted by the various parallel routes running along the northern edge of the Chilterns. Here it is very clear that the Way was originally a mile wide.

> The Icknield Way certainly did not begin life as the road or bridlepath or green lane we now see … Icknield was then … an intertwining of many paths … (Crosher, 1973.)

Eventually these have been confined into the two, three or four parallel tracks visible today;

some are still routes, whether roads, tracks or paths, whilst others survive only as hedges or boundaries.

Icknield Way is essentially a continuation of the Great Ridgeway, but there are two important differences. The first is that most of its tracks are at the foot of the scarp – and it is odd that this section of the long-distance path is still referred to as the Ridgeway (Fig. 7). The second difference is that the Romans improved many lengths of one of the old tracks, essentially making it into a Roman road. Many later documentary references are to Icknield *Street*, a word which often denotes a Roman road. It is dealt with in this chapter as the origins of the route as a whole are clearly pre-Roman.

Starting from Goring, the first 9½ miles (15 km) were not improved by the Romans and the modern Ridgeway footpath takes an entirely different route until reaching the foot of Swyncombe Downs, having covered some 12 miles (20 km) to reach the same point. The Way

5 *A typical view of the Ridgeway long-distance footpath near Wantage, now enclosed by hedges.*

passes through a gap in Grim's Ditch, one of many prehistoric earthworks built across the ridgeways, and immediately there are a number of parallel tracks which are the sole remnants of this former wide route (Figs. 8 and 9).

The Romanised route is described in great detail by the Viatores (1964). A possible sign of Roman work is a straight alignment from Turners Court to Lewknor, but the first good evidence is the alignment of the B4009, running north-west from Watlington to within a mile of Lewknor. The Roman road is then lost until it reappears north of Lewknor on a new alignment; here it is seen as a track or path parallel to the modern B road for 3 miles (5 km), until it is joined by that road at Chinnor (Fig. 10). In this length there are still three parallel

tracks: the northernmost is the Romanised Lower Icknield Way; the middle is the modern B road, the sole remnant of the old wide route still surviving as a through road. The southernmost track is now called the Upper Icknield Way, and is followed here by the modern long-distance path. None of the routes runs along the ridge of the Chilterns at this point, though it has been suggested that there may well have been such a route. The routes which survive are clearly very different from the ridgeways of Wessex.

This duplication of routes continues along much of the line of the Icknield Way. The modern Ridgeway footpath ends at Beacon Hill, near Ivinghoe, whilst the Romanised Icknield Way continues through Tring,

Dunstable (where it crosses Watling Street), Luton, Letchworth, Baldock and Royston, to a junction north of the Roman town of Great Chesterford. It then continues by way of Newmarket and Thetford to the Wash, its final section lying parallel to the later Roman Peddars Way. Why the Romans should have improved the track, and also built a new route alongside for almost 40 miles (64 km) is a mystery; it certainly shows that having good routes to the Wash was important to them.

The Icknield Way is one of the most complicated of all routes in Britain – virtually any route roughly parallel to the ridge may well be a remnant of the old mile-wide way along which people used to travel. Some of the surviving routes of the Icknield Way have been straightened by the enclosure surveyors (see Chapter 8). Others have main roads running along them (for example the A505 from Baldock to Royston, and the A11 from Great Chesterford to Newmarket), whilst others are simply green lanes or footpaths, or have gone out of use altogether. The modern long-distance footpath is just as much a part of all this history as any other, even though, as a through route, it was created only in 1973.

OTHER PREHISTORIC TRACKS

Of the many tracks identified in Wessex, the Harrow Way is one of the more important, as it led eastwards from the Stonehenge area to join what later became known as the Pilgrims' Way which runs along the North Downs to the east coast of Kent (see Chapter 3). This road competes with the main Ridgeway for the title of the oldest road in Britain; its name probably means 'hard way', referring to the chalk underfoot (Timperley & Brill, 1983). From Farnham, two routes have been identified (main and summer ways?) which joined beyond Basingstoke; the track then passed just to the north of Andover and is followed closely by the modern A303 to Amesbury and Stonehenge (Wright, 1988). It may well have crossed the

6 *Rocque's map of Berkshire (1761) shows 'The Ridge Way' on the downs above the Vale of White Horse. (Reproduced by courtesy of H. Margary.)*

7 *A Ridgeway long-distance footpath sign, confusingly seen on the Icknield Way.*

Ridgeway close to the place where the A350 crosses the A303, between Warminster and Shaftesbury, before going on further west (see Fig. 2).

As noted above, all the possible prehistoric tracks are difficult to authenticate, and outside southern England only a handful have a demonstrable claim to antiquity. There certainly were many prehistoric tracks in the north and west of Britain, but perhaps they had less traffic, were less prominent in the landscape and have survived less well than those tracks on the chalk downlands. The problem with such routes is that there has been a tendency to assume that any track running across isolated high ridges and passing the odd tumulus must automatically have prehistoric origins, just as had been assumed (with rather more certainty) in southern England. Although definite proof is almost inevitably missing, several deserve a brief mention.

The Exmoor Ridgeway, which runs across the moor north of the B3223 and B3358, has

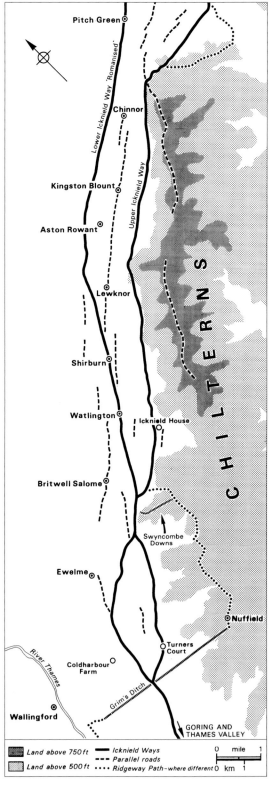

8 *Surviving lines of the former mile-wide Icknield Way beneath the Chilterns; one line was Romanised, and another is now the long-distance Ridgeway footpath, though the latter takes an entirely new route in places.*

9 *One of the remnants of the former mile-wide Icknield Way running beneath the Chiltern scarp near Lewknor. It is crossed at this point by the M40; here one of Britain's newest roads crosses one of the oldest.*

been tentatively identified as a Bronze Age track, apparently also known to and used by the Saxons. Perhaps similar in date is the Kerry Hills Ridgeway which leads into the much later town of Bishop's Castle in the mid-Welsh borders; it has been described as the oldest road in Wales. It was certainly important in the days of the drovers, when it was one of the main routes into England (see Chapter 5). It is associated with several other high-level routes, including the Clun-Clee Ridgeway and the 'Portway' along the top of the Long Mynd (Portway is a Saxon word for an important road leading to a market or port). Walks along both these ridge routes are described in Dunn (1986). The Exmoor ridgeway is outlined in Toulson

10 *The Romanised Icknield Way now changes from a field track to a metalled road on entering the village of Chinnor.*

(1983) and Hannigan (1994). Several Bronze Age tracks on Dartmoor are also suggested in Toulson (1984).

In Derbyshire, several routes between the major monuments have been tentatively identified, including a route from the hillfort on Mam Tor, running to the south past three other forts. It is known as the Old Portway, and its origins may well be contemporary with the use of the forts. It has, of course, been much altered subsequently, notably during its later history as a packhorse route (Dodd, 1980).

Into this well populated land with its network of tracks came the Romans, who were to impose a new and largely independent system of engineered roads. The old main tracks which had served the British for so long generally went in directions of little use to the Romans. They were also clearly physically inadequate for the new military and trading needs and many must have gone out of use. However, the local tracks from one farmstead to the next must have continued to be used, and many have no doubt remained in use ever since.

Chapter Two

ROMAN ROADS

THE ROMAN INVASION of Britain in AD 43 is one of the most important turning points in British history. Not only did it herald almost four hundred years of Roman rule, but the Romans were also to leave a legacy of forts, towns and roads which have influenced the urban structure, road system and landscape to this day. Indeed, many British towns and roads have been built on top of or alongside their Roman predecessors. By AD 47 the Romans had advanced as far as a line from Exeter to Lincoln, and the remarkably straight Foss Way was probably built as a strategic road to serve the Roman legions. It took the Romans over 45 years to bring the rest of England and Wales firmly under their control; this was finally achieved by Agricola who conquered Wales and northern England by AD 80. The attempt to conquer Scotland was unsuccessful. After several forays, the border was established along Hadrian's Wall; it was begun in the 120s, and became the permanent frontier from 163.

In studying Roman roads it is not possible to agree with Margary (1973) that 'the roads were laid out as a carefully planned system'. On the contrary, there was much piecemeal development, with each road being built for a specific purpose at a particular date; two or three adjacent roads might have been laid out in conjunction with each other, but clearly there was no overall master plan. In order to have undertaken such a plan the Romans would have needed a detailed map of much of Britain; there is no evidence that such a map ever existed. Having said that, it is evident that

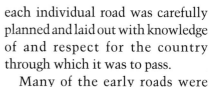

each individual road was carefully planned and laid out with knowledge of and respect for the country through which it was to pass.

Many of the early roads were clearly military in nature, linking one fort to the next, first to allow the rapid and easy movement of troops and provisions, and then to subdue, conquer and control the country. This is especially true of roads in Wales and the north of England, areas which were under army control for many years. These military roads were imposed on the landscape, and they took little account of what was there already, except on the rare occasions when they improved existing tracks. When conditions became more settled and trade increased in importance, many of the major trading routes must have been between the existing forts and towns, and thus along the roads which had already been built.

Some later roads were built primarily for trade, especially in the south-eastern part of the country, which was soon under civil control. Johnston (1979) argues that there is a clear distinction between the planned military roads, and those which grew by 'natural growth'. But there are mysteries too. Some obvious links were never built, and Roman towns failed to grow at many major junctions, such as Old Sarum and Badbury Rings.

The total length of Roman roads will probably never be known. One reason for this is that new sections are continually being found; another is that there was a hierarchy of roads, built to different standards and widths. The main roads were the well-built highways

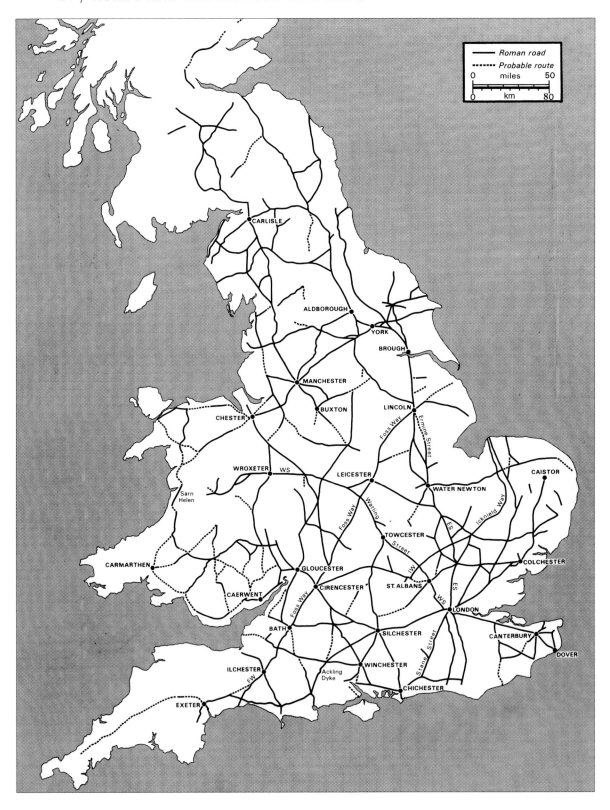

funded by the military or the state. Next in the scale came the local roads financed by each district. Finally there were the private roads serving individual estates, farms, villas or mines, or dividing up agricultural land for new settlement. The major Roman roads vary greatly in their importance and in their levels of engineering. Only the more important roads are likely to survive and be traceable; thus we can reconstruct only the network of main roads with any degree of certainty (Fig. 11). This network probably totalled close to 10,000 miles (16,000 km).

The minor road system has generally been forgotten or ignored, largely because of the immense difficulty of seeing it. Hoskins (1955) said that

> We have been bemused too long by the great military roads of the Romans and have not given enough thought and research to the local 'economic' roads ...

and Hooke (1977) has commented that

> the network of [main] Roman roads thrown across the West Midland countryside ... was obviously inadequate to serve the needs of such a region.

There must have been a great mileage of local tracks between settlements and fields, which had very little (if any) engineering or surfacing; many were no doubt pre-Roman roads in origin. It may be possible to distinguish them from the main Roman roads by the terms used in Anglo-Saxon and later charters – Roman roads are usually termed *straets*, whilst the minor tracks are *paeths* or *wegs*.

There is no way of estimating the mileage of the minor roads and tracks, but many lanes and farm tracks must have been in use in Roman times, even though they may now not look in the least like what we think of as 'typical' Roman roads. Occasionally some

11 *The network of main Roman roads; many lengths are uncertain or missing. (After Margary, 1973.)*

evidence of these local tracks remains, even if only on aerial photographs where they can be seen perhaps leading to a Roman villa, fields or some other site. Taylor (1979) gives examples of minor Roman roads in Dorset; three tracks near Maiden Newton can be seen to link several Roman fields and farmsteads, whilst near Milton Abbas four tracks lead out from a Roman village, two surviving as embanked holloways and one as a terraceway.

The Romans applied their love of straight lines to the laying out of fields and field roads. The process by which land was divided up by surveyors is called 'centuriation', as it was based on multiples of a hundred. The basic unit of length was the *actus* of 120 Roman feet (116 statute feet; 35m), and plot dimensions were made up of various multiples of it. Margary (1948) demonstrated the evidence for such deliberate planning near the village of Ripe, east of Lewes (Fig. 12). At first sight, such patterns might appear to be those of Parliamentary enclosure (see Chapter 8), but there was no such enclosure here, and the layout is Roman. These lanes, with their striking rectangular pattern, are essentially the 'occupation roads' of Roman times. However, the pattern has strayed somewhat from the original, just as one might expect after almost 2,000 years; such changes have not occurred in the 200 years since enclosure (Fig. 13). Centuriation has been noted elsewhere, including Rochester, as well as at such unlikely spots as east Manchester and around Penrith.

Most of the field evidence of minor Roman roads no longer exists; few of these tracks were engineered or surfaced and they may well have been ploughed out, or have been in use ever since. In such cases any Roman origins are impossible to see or prove and the vast majority of such lesser features of the Roman landscape have long since disappeared. The ploughing up of the downlands of southern England during the Second World War certainly destroyed some of these tracks. Of

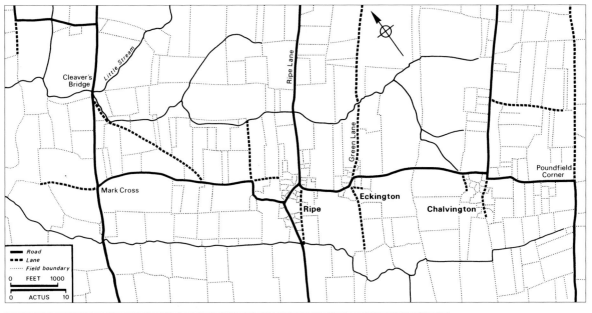

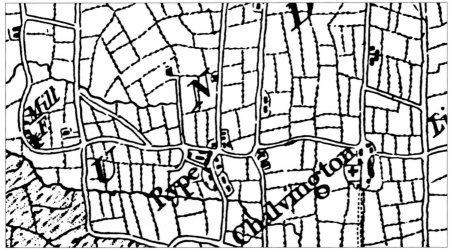

12 and **13** *The surviving network of Roman roads and fields around Ripe in Sussex. The pattern of centuriation is shown both by a recent map, and by Gardner and Gream's map of the county (1795) (left). (Reproduced by courtesy of H. Margary.)*

necessity, therefore, this chapter concentrates on the major routes.

The more important Roman roads vary a good deal in their present appearance, not least because of differences in their construction. Typically they have an agger (the raised central ridge), usually bounded by ditches on either side. Local materials were used in construction, whether beach pebbles, gravel or quarried rock. Their width varies a good deal; the agger may be between 10 and 25 feet (3-8m) across, and the ditches may be 15 to 85 feet (5-26m) apart.

However, the agger of a major road such as Ermine Street can be up to 50ft (15m) wide, and 5 feet (1.5m) in height. These roads vary quite considerably along their length. They are embanked in some places and not in others, and they may not be metalled throughout. These inconsistencies seem to have been the result both of different engineers building different sections, as well as the different requirements for each part of the route. The less engineered sections of a road may now be much less obvious in the landscape. Many of the

Roman mountain roads were evidently not metalled, and only seem to have received any attention from the engineers when the need for their use arose. Such roads are often little more than terraces cut into hillsides, and can be particularly difficult to trace and prove as Roman.

It is of course a well-known fact (at least according to Sellar and Yeatman's *1066 and All That)* that 'the Roman roads ran absolutely straight in all directions and all led to Rome'! This glorious oversimplification is not totally removed from the truth. Roman roads were *direct* rather than straight, and usually proceeded in a series of straight alignments. They sometimes aim from a great distance directly for their goal, but may divert in order to avoid boggy ground, awkward river crossings, or some other difficulty. When confronted by a steep hill, they either embarked on a set of zigzags, took a more circuitous route, or simply went straight up the slope. Steep slopes were not a problem, as these roads were designed principally for the rapid movement of men, horses and pack animals, rather than for the passage of laden carts.

The use of straight alignments was fundamentally a matter of simplicity and convenience for the surveyors and engineers; yet they chose their routes with great skill, taking care to use the natural routes through the landscape wherever possible. The surveyors clearly undertook a general survey of the whole route first, looking for the best lines. It is simply not known how the long alignments were made; the Foss Way runs for over 200 miles (322 km), yet is never more than 8 miles (13 km) from the direct line between Axminster and Lincoln.

The detached alignments of Stane Street form a rather different, but equally good example (see below, and Fig. 16). Changes of alignment were often made on high ground, so that the next section of road could more easily be laid out. There is a great contrast between the long straight lengths such as those taken by Watling Street across the Midlands (now the A5), and the much more pragmatic design of Roman roads through the mountainous areas of Wales or the Lake District. Yet even in the hills the roads always tend to proceed in short straight stretches wherever possible.

Not all straight roads are of Roman origin; many more were created by Parliamentary enclosure in the years around 1800, but these are usually obvious both in the landscape and in the written record, and they never connect one Roman site with another (see Chapter 8). The rare exception to this is when a Roman road was made part of an enclosure road system (see Figs. 28 and 105).

TRACING ROMAN ROADS

There is still great scope for the Roman road hunter, whether amateur or professional, as many roads have yet to be fully traced. It has to be said, though, that most of the 'easy' Roman roads have already been found. The standard technique involves historical and cartographic research followed by field observation, backed up by proper excavation only if necessary (Bagshawe, 1979). There is one piece of contemporary written evidence for Roman roads, namely the *Antonine Itinerary*, which is a list of the main roads of the empire – 15 routes are given in Britain, most of which have now been traced on the ground.

The first step in any research is to obtain a description and map of known Roman roads; Margary (1973) is the basic starting point, but he deals only with the most important roads and is now many years out of date. So the next step is to check in local libraries to see what recent research has been done. There may well be a local archaeological society or journal, and there is usually also a well known 'Roman road expert' in each area. The Archaeology Branch of the Ordnance Survey also keeps detailed records, as do various local archaeological units. All this research will reveal many gaps in the known network.

14 *The dual carriageway of the A419 north of Swindon is directly on top of the Roman road from Silchester to Cirencester. The road has probably been a landscape feature for almost two thousand years.*

Several areas have already received detailed treatment, including the Weald by Margary himself (1948), and the south-east Midlands by him and a group of his enthusiastic followers (Viatores, 1964), but much remains to be done. The present author was amazed to find, over twenty years ago, in researching the Roman roads of the Lake District, that no one had previously tried to reconstruct the network in that well-known and much written-about corner of Britain.

In order to understand the Roman road system in an area, it is important to determine when each fort and town was established, as the main roads to each place would have been built at the same time as the settlements, if not before. Indeed, in the early stages of the military occupation it would have been normal practice to build the main penetrative roads first, to back

up the invasion, with troops living in temporary camps. Some forts were evidently built as afterthoughts, placed on roads at an appropriate place for victualling, usually a day's march apart (about 10-15 miles; 16-24 km). On the other hand, many forts later went out of use, and the roads to them decayed or were replaced.

Next, maps should be consulted; virtually any old map of an area may be of use. Eighteenth-century county maps and early editions of the Ordnance Survey one-inch map are good starting points for getting a general view of a route, but detailed work requires the 6-inch and 25-inch OS maps. The latter maps were first surveyed in the second half of the 19th century and they show field and parish boundaries and place-names in considerable detail. They also show roads before 20th-century alterations, as well as features no longer evident in the landscape, for example those which have been built over or destroyed by ploughing. Furthermore they may be freely copied as they are out of copyright. Aerial photographs, if available, may also be of great use.

The importance of parish boundaries in tracing Roman roads may not be immediately obvious. Most seem to have been created after the Romans had left, in the long and often unsettled period known as the Dark Ages. When people were choosing sites for their farms or hamlets, they clearly avoided the Roman roads, probably to keep out of the way of any marauders; the aggers of the roads would also form obvious boundaries. Consequently, throughout large areas of England, parish boundaries follow Roman roads. Watling Street (A5) has virtually no early settlements on it, and is a parish boundary for most of its length. However, a straight road with a parish boundary running along it is not automatically Roman; features which are specifically Roman must be sought as confirmation.

The next step is to note any obvious Roman detail, whether known roads, milestones, towns, forts, burials or villas, and to add the various place-names (and field names) which are associated with Roman sites and roads. Roman roads may be indicated by Street (also Stretton, Stratford), Gate (meaning road), Ford, Stone or Stane (referring to the metalling), Ridge, Ridgeway, Causeway, Coldharbour or Caldecot. Most of these are self-explanatory but the last two are not; these place-names are commonly found close to Roman roads and probably referred to roadside shelters.

With the aid of a ruler, extending whatever short alignments have been found, it is often possible to see much longer alignments of roads, hedges, paths or boundaries at this stage. The search is simply for a series of short straight alignments connecting one Roman site to another.

If a new alignment is found, then it is time to get into the field to see if there are any

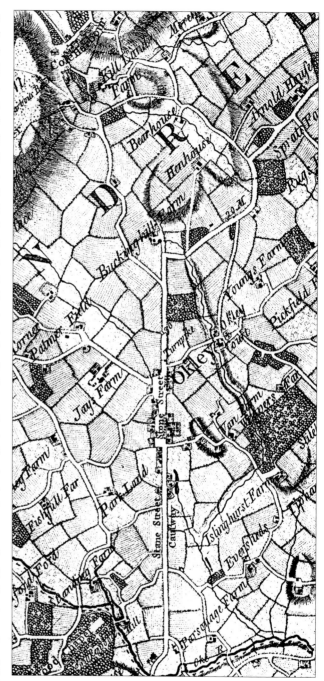

15 Rocque's map of Surrey (1768) shows Stane Street clearly where it passes through Ockley; this short section is now the A29. To the north, the road disappears, but there is a 'Cole Harbour' place-name at the top of the extract. (Reproduced by courtesy of H. Margary.)

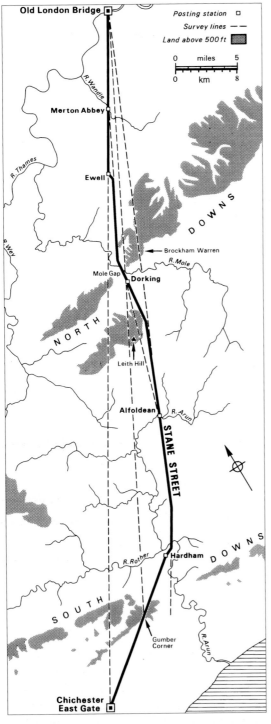

16 *The alignments of Stane Street between London and Chichester display the great accuracy of Roman road surveying over long distances.*

remains on the ground; indeed the main evidence for the Roman road system has always lain in the landscape itself. This can be the most exciting part of the process, for the options open to the Roman surveyor should start to become clearer – features which may not be shown on the map (such as minor steep slopes, marshy ground or former marshy ground) can be seen at first hand. A good imagination is needed to try to envisage what the countryside may have been like two thousand years ago. Of course, many Roman roads are still in use, and the original engineering may now lie beneath tarmac (Fig. 14). Some roads may have been obscured by centuries of erosion, traffic or soil movement, removed by ploughing or tree planting, whilst others may now simply be inaccessible due to unhelpful landowners. It is surprising, though, how many Roman roads are still rights of way.

The final proof of Roman date may require a section to be dug, but professional help *must* be sought as digging is destructive and a bad excavation may destroy valuable evidence. There will always be lengths where there is no physical evidence, and obtaining absolute proof of a Roman road for any great length is very difficult; a string of detached observations will often be the best that can be obtained. An excellent example of long and patient detective work is the discovery of the Roman route across the northern Lake District from Penrith to Workington by Martin Allen (1994).

There are so many Roman roads that it is clearly impossible to mention more than a few here. There are many local studies, such as Graystone (1992, 1996) for Lancashire. A more popular approach, covering the whole country, is by Livingstone (1995). What follows is a rather arbitrary selection, but they are chosen to illustrate the different types of road, the different features which they exhibit and the problems involved in tracing them.

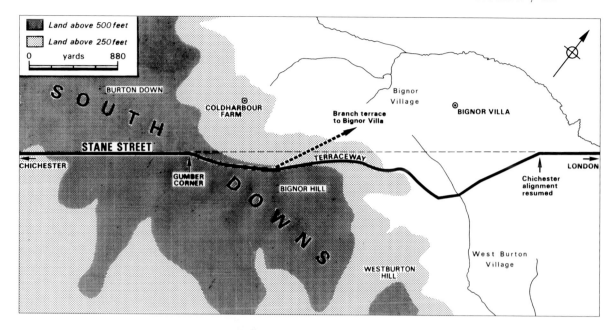

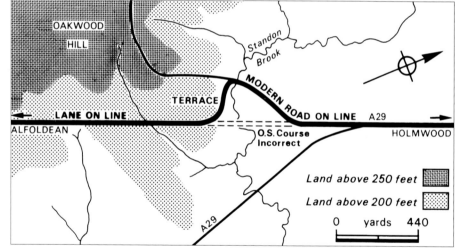

17a and **b** *Two examples of the way in which Roman road builders adapted the direct line of Stane Street to meet local conditions. (After Margary, 1948.)*

STANE STREET AND THE WEALD

Stane Street is probably the best known Roman road south of London, it connects that city to Chichester, then the tribal capital of Sussex. Its name refers to its stony surface, and it is first referred to as 'Stanstret' in 1270; it is clearly shown on Rocque's map of Surrey (1768) (Fig. 15). It was the subject of a very readable but rather inaccurate book by Hilaire Belloc (1913). The route is described in detail by Margary (1948); much of it remains in use. The route has only nine alignments, of which three can be described as major. The first alignment from London heads directly for Chichester's east gate, which is 56 miles (90 km) distant and obviously out of sight; it maintains this line as far as Ewell. Further south a 12-mile (20 km) section points directly back towards London (Fig. 16). How these detached but precisely surveyed alignments were laid out remains a mystery.

On the ground, however, the road frequently deviates from the precise line in response to local topography:

> such modifications of a major alignment occur very frequently ... and a slavish adherence to a rigid line is certainly not to be looked for if the ground does not favour it. (Margary, 1948.)

From London the road leaves the first alignment at Ewell in order to take advantage of travelling on the chalk for an extra 3 miles (5 km). The road passes through the Mole Gap at Dorking, and leaves the precise alignment for a mile; here it

> changes abruptly to a terrace around the head of the combe ... Even in this sinuous course the famous Roman straightness is not forgotten ... [it is] a flexible line of straight pieces. (Johnston, 1979.)

Nearer Chichester, it leaves the alignment again, this time for almost 2 miles (3 km) at Bignor Hill; it was built as a terraceway to tackle the hill, and deviates by up to 400 yards (365m) from the direct line. Margary also demonstrates that the course then shown on the Ordnance Survey maps is incorrect in places. At Oakwood Hill, north-west of Horsham, the OS map assumed that the road went straight down a steep bank and across a stream. In fact the correct line involved a diversion to cross 200 yards (180m) upstream; this line is followed by the parish boundary (Fig. 17a and b).

Margary (1948) also describes a very different group of roads in the Kentish Weald, south of the section of Watling Street between Rochester and Canterbury. Although so close to London, this was a remote and difficult area in Roman times, only thinly populated. Margary points out that although these roads are

> distinctly Roman in parts of their layout and construction, they are yet very imperfect in the accuracy of the alignments ... a circumstance which suggests a relatively late date for their construction ...

The main road was probably built for commercial rather than military reasons, in particular to serve the Wealden iron industry in the area around Battle. At its southern end the road probably led to long silted-up ports, such as at Bodiam.

Some parts of the route are now overlain by modern roads, notably the A229, through Staplehurst to Sissinghurst, but elsewhere the route can be traced by aggers, holloways, cuttings, zigzags or merely as hedgerows along the line of the road. Only rarely is it followed by parish boundaries, suggesting that it ceased to be an important feature in the landscape after the Romans left. In several places Margary again found that the old OS alignments were wrong. A peculiarity of the roads in this area is their use of iron slag as road metalling.

WATLING STREET

There are numerous roads now called Watling Street, the most important and best known of which led from Dover through Canterbury, London, St Albans, Dunstable and Towcester to meet the Foss Way at High Cross. It was later continued to the Welsh border at Wroxeter from where another road (the 'Western Watling Street') linked Caerleon and Chester. It remained important even in the 'Dark Ages' when much of it formed the boundary between the English and Danish Mercian kingdoms. Most of it is still in use, notably as the A2 and A5, and thus much of the Roman engineering has been destroyed. Occasionally, though, the modern road is not always directly on top of its Roman precursor.

The section from London to Towcester is given by three routes in the *Antonine Itinerary*, and it is described in great detail by the Viatores (1964). Edgware Road marks its course out of London, and only two main alignments were needed to cover the 19 miles (30 km) to the important town of Verulamium, just west of the later St Albans. The route is now largely overlain by the A5, including the dog-leg at Elstree, yet the agger is still visible in a few places, despite the continuing use of the road and the great number of buildings constructed alongside.

> Because so much of this road has remained in continuous service as one of the chief thoroughfares of England, and now carries an immensely heavy traffic, its form has been greatly modified for long distances, first by turnpike works in the coaching era, and more recently by large-scale widenings. There is thus little chance of seeing any relics of its original state, and all that can be observed now is the layout of the alignments and they way in which parish and county boundaries frequently follow it. (Margary, 1973)

Nevertheless, the route is easily followed by car, and the rare occasions where the old route still survives can easily be found and visited.

Beyond Verulamium, the road had to find an easy route across the Chilterns, and in two places the original line and the A5 part company. These are from Friar's Wash to Markyate (north of Flamstead), and again from Markyate to the outskirts of Dunstable, where it crosses the Romanised Icknield Way (see Chapter 1). North of Dunstable, the Roman road took a gentle zigzag to cross the final chalk ridge at Puddlehill, with gradients of up to 1 in 8; a short section of the Roman summit cutting still survives (Viatores, 1964).

THE VIATORES

This group of investigators concentrated their efforts on the area bounded by London, Silchester, High Cross and Godmanchester (Viatores, 1964). They were able to give immense detail about the main roads, and even corrected portions of roads which were already well known by the time they wrote. Their work has been criticised for the inclusion of roads of doubtful Roman origin; nevertheless, they described an extensive radial system of roads from Verulamium, plus several long distance routes. In addition they revealed some of the elusive local roads and these are much more difficult to trace and prove as Roman; they were never as well engineered, and were less likely

to have had long alignments. Of the 49 roads in their survey, totalling 850 miles (1,370 km), only 11 were known previously.

Their major single discovery was a 65 mile (105 km) road running north-east from Dorchester to Ermine Street, which had almost entirely disappeared from the landscape; its discovery began by the checking of a single place-name (Causeway End at Wootton, Bedford). The route is remarkably direct, and it lies parallel to, and between, the Foss Way and Icknield Way, but, unlike them, it has numerous changes of alignment and diversions. It does, though, have the classic feature of being made up of straight stretches with changes of alignment on higher ground. Other evidence included medieval road names, place-names, a paved ford, plus various Roman sites and finds. It is obviously no longer a through route, but many minor roads still use it for short stretches. There are several good surviving sections of agger (though rarely more than 20 feet (6m) wide), but often it is represented by nothing more than hedges, parish boundaries, or as a footpath or holloway. There was a settlement where it crosses Akeman Street. It crosses Watling Street at Little Brickhill, and ends at Alconbury where it joins Ermine Street. This was clearly one of the later cross-country routes built for economic reasons.

FOSS WAY

This road (sometimes spelt Fosse) was constructed by about AD 47, and it used to be thought that it was the north-west frontier of Roman Britain at that time, partly due to its (later) name, meaning 'ditch road'. However, there were several forts in front of that line, and it is perhaps best seen as a strategic road, allowing rearward communication between the various legions. A curious feature is that its surveyed line is virtually parallel to two sections of Stane Street, over 85 miles (135 km) away (Jones and Mattingly, 1990). Most of the

18   *An unclassified modern road along the line of the Foss(e) Way, just south of its junction with Watling Street (A5) at High Cross.*

Foss Way is still visible in the landscape, whether as a modern road or lane, or just as a path or hedgerow. It runs for 208 miles (335 km) from Axmouth via Axminster, Ilchester, Bath, Cirencester, Moreton-in-Marsh, High Cross, Leicester and Newark to Lincoln, always within a few miles of the overall alignment; this remarkable directness is a testament to Roman surveying.

It is no longer a through route, though modern major roads follow it for some length, for example from south of Ilchester to Bath (A303, A37, A367), from south of Cirencester to Halford (A429), and finally for 58 miles (93 km) from just south of Leicester to Lincoln (A46). But most of these modern major roads are going across the line of the Foss Way, and only follow it where it suits them. An interesting section lies immediately to the south of the

A5 at High Cross, where it is now a minor road (with a couple of miles as a B road) for over 27 miles (43 km) towards Stow-on-the-Wold. It is clearly signposted as the 'Fosse Way', its lack of traffic is in sharp contrast to the busy A5 (Fig. 18). A walk along one of the sections which survives only as a path, south-west of Cirencester, is described by Dunn (1986).

WELSH ROADS

The Romans took a long time to complete their conquest of Wales, and the road system must have emerged over quite an extended period. The 'Western Watling Street' along the border is certainly earlier in date than the roads connected with the invasion of Anglesey in AD 60, or the general conquest of Wales in the mid-70s. Wales had a long period of military control, and there is thus a dense scattering of some three dozen forts. The detailed chronology of these forts has been worked out; most were occupied only during the early stages of conquest and pacification. After about AD 125 only a few forts continued to be occupied (Jones and Mattingly, 1990). Thus the road network expanded and contracted in response to these changing needs; many roads were in use for only a few decades.

The Roman road system in Wales is still imperfectly known, chiefly through lack of investigation. However, it can be more difficult to trace roads through hilly areas as the roads were narrower than in the lowlands, have few long alignments and both surfacing and good aggers are rare. The area with the best developed road system is in South Wales, designed to subdue the tribe of the Silures – for example, roads fan out in six directions from the fort at Brecon. But elsewhere in Wales there were few Roman roads, though these were evidently planned with great care to encircle the central hills. There were legionary fortresses along the border at Chester, Wroxeter, Usk and Caerleon, and a rectangle of roads linked that border with Brecon and Carmarthen in the south and with Caernarfon in the north. The road running down the western edge of this rectangle is known as the Sarn Helen (Colyer, 1984) (Fig. 19).

The road's name probably means 'Road of the Legion' (Sarn-y-Lleng), though other more romantic explanations have been suggested. In fact, the name Sarn Helen is applied to many vaguely Roman looking roads throughout Wales. The route of the Sarn Helen is still uncertain in many places, notably in the middle part of its course. It starts in the Conwy valley, and one of the first clear sections is near Ffestiniog, where it is seen as a 9 foot (3m) wide track north of the Ffestiniog to Bala road. South of Ffestiniog the Roman road is not overlain by the A487, but lies a little to the east, first as a lane and then as a terrace on the hillside. Of the central section from Pennal to Lledrod, Margary (1973) said:

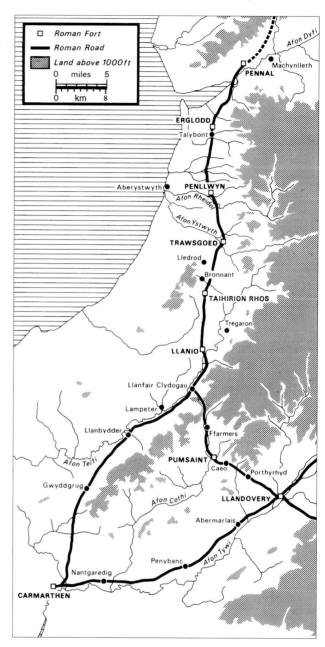

19 *The Sarn Helen (from Pennal to Llanio) and associated Roman roads in west Wales. (After Colyer, 1984.)*

If there have been doubtful portions of Sarn Helen already described it should be said at once that this section of it is still extremely uncertain ... and it can only warrant inclusion here because it is virtually certain that there must have been a through road ...

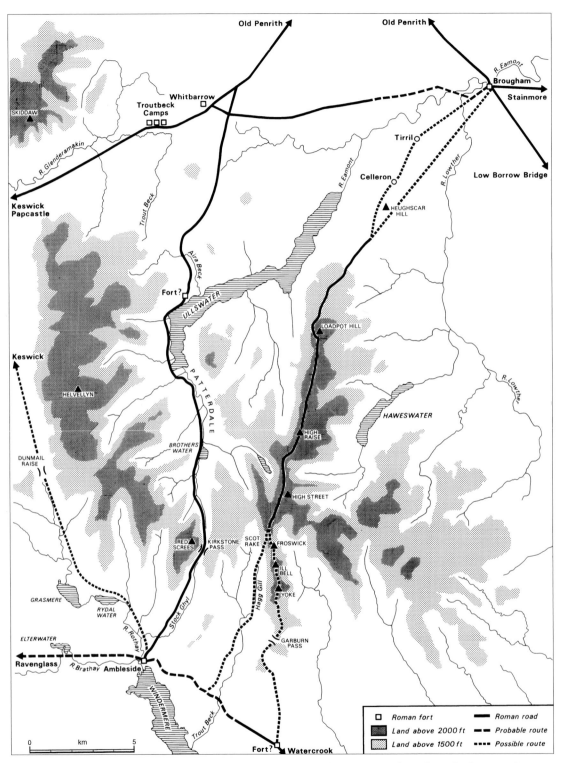

20 *High Street and the Kirkstone Pass Roman roads; High Street may have been little more than a temporary route, soon replaced by the lower and easier route over Kirkstone Pass.*

The whole of the route south of Pennal is dealt with in great detail by Colyer (1984). He clearly points out that there is still no definite proof that the roads he describes are Roman; very few roads here have been excavated.

> This part of Cardiganshire is criss-crossed by scores, if not hundreds of miles of trackways of uncertain vintage, and it is hardly surprising that other courses for *Sarn Helen* have been postulated.

Writing later than Margary, and with much more detailed local knowledge, Colyer was able to incorporate the recent discoveries of forts which the roads served. The most important of these were the fortlet at Erglodd and the large fort at Penllwyn, 3 miles (5 km) from Aberystwyth, overlooking the river Rheidol, both discovered only in the 1970s. These discoveries fixed two more places through which the road must have run. The next fort is at Trawsgoed on the river Ystwyth; Colyer suggests a route further inland than did Margary, which climbs to join the A485 south of Bronnant, where there was yet another fort. Margary had thought that the present main road from Lledrod was the likely route. The A road coincides with the Roman line for 1½ miles (2 km), and then the

B4578 takes over, leading directly to the next fort at Llanio. Throughout this difficult area, locating the forts has been the clue to finding the road which must have connected them.

South of Llanio, the Sarn Helen divides at Llanfair Clydogau, with the western branch leading to Carmarthen, closely followed by the present A485. The other branch led to Llandovery, going across the hills to Pumsaint, where the Roman fort which guarded the gold mines at Dolaucothi was discovered only in 1972. It then went via Caeo and Porthyrhyd to Llandovery; a route which was to be used again by the drovers many centuries later (see Chapter 5).

LAKELAND ROADS

High Street is probably the best known Roman road in the Lake District. Its route along the top of the mountain ridge of the same name is spectacular, keeping at a height of over 1,500ft (460m) for some 10 miles (16 km), and reaching almost 2,700ft (825m) at the summit (Hindle, 1998a). This central section of the route is very clear on the ground. From High Raise the road runs northwards in a straight line along the crest of the ridge to Loadpot Hill. Here it

21 *The agger of High Street at the northern end of the summit section.*

22 *The confirmation of a Roman road over Kirkstone Pass, seen as the shelf on the right-hand side of the valley, has cast doubt on the importance of High Street, which lies only a few miles to the east.*

changes alignment, and aims directly for the fort at Brougham. There is a well defined agger, and much of this alignment runs closely parallel to a parish boundary (Figs. 20 and 21).

There are many difficulties associated with this route, however. Between the known northern end of the summit section and Brougham the evidence is very confusing, and no clear route has been found; much of this area has been enclosed, and more recently deep ploughed. To the south of the summit its course has never been established at all; its obvious destination would have been the fort at Ambleside, but a possible fort has been discovered at Broadgate, east of Windermere, at the very southern end of the High Street ridge. The question also has to be asked whether the Romans would have been able to use horses regularly on a road which has no water supplies for at least 10 miles (16 km). The final doubt is caused by the discovery

of a Roman road from Ambleside northwards over the Kirkstone Pass, along Ullswater, and then via Whitbarrow to Old Penrith (Fig. 22) (Richardson & Allan, 1990). Much of this route is only a few miles to the west of High Street, and, being much lower, has no lack of water. Why should there be two parallel Roman roads here?

Perhaps the answer is that High Street was simply an old ridge route which the Romans improved in part, as an early temporary military link between Brougham and Ambleside; it would certainly have been an obvious route to choose. But in the long run it was not needed, and never became an important route. The reason why the route at the southern end has not been found may well be that the Romans never engineered this section at all.

The road from Kendal to Ravenglass also traverses the Lakeland fells, but it could hardly

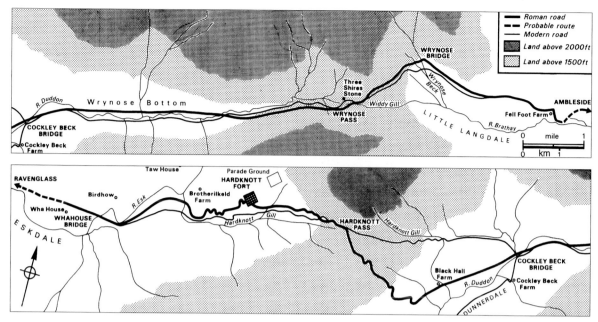

23 *The Roman road over Hardknott and Wrynose passes is still clear on the ground, but the links to Ravenglass and Ambleside have proved elusive.*

be more different. We know that it was an important route as it is listed as the final two stages of a route in the *Antonine Itinerary*. It traverses difficult terrain, and there must have been compelling reasons for building it. The road may have been built to isolate the Britons of southern Lakeland (there are no known Roman roads or forts in Lakeland south of this line), or simply to complete the road network by providing a second link to the southernmost fort along the Cumbrian coast. The idea that it was built in preparation for an invasion of Ireland is no longer supported.

In terms of surviving field evidence, most of the route has disappeared (Hindle, 1998a). The best surviving section is through the hills, over the two passes, where it can be followed almost continuously for 6 miles (10 km) (Fig. 23). The road first appears on Wrynose Pass above the modern road, as a terrace on the hillside, up to 18 feet (5.5m) wide. The two routes meet at the top of the pass, but then diverge, with the Roman road again above the present one. Once in Wrynose Bottom, the Roman road is very

clear as a 24 foot (7m) wide causeway on the north side of the stream, complete with kerb stones. Beyond Cockley Beck Bridge it is represented by the track to Black Hall. For the ascent of Hardknott Pass the Romans chose an entirely different route to the present road; their route is still a right of way, and is clearly shown on the OS map. It has a different summit, but the two roads join briefly for the start of the descent; however, where the modern road makes its notorious steep zigzag, the Romans went straight on, heading for their fort, perched high above Eskdale (Fig. 24). The road was engineered to a high standard; it was never less than 15 feet (5 m) wide, even in the most difficult places:

> it shows a considerable adaptation to the physical topography with cuttings, terraces, curves and straight alignments, all built to reduce to a minimum the considerable problems for road users. (Taylor, 1979.)

Below the fort the Roman road disappears in the fields and the rest of its route to Ravenglass is elusive.

24 *The Roman road descending the western side of Hardknott Pass went straight on at this point, heading for the fort. The parade ground above the fort can be seen in the middle distance, left.*

OTHER ROADS

This is a brief list of some of the other well known Roman roads, concentrating on those which have acquired specific names:

Ackling Dyke: Old Sarum (Salisbury) to Dorchester. A massive agger can be seen in several places, notably where the road crosses the Dorset Downs of Cranborne Chase. The well preserved agger south of Woodyates, 10 miles (16 km) south-west of Salisbury on the A354, is best observed on Bottlebush Down, where the Dyke is crossed by the B3081 (Fig. 25).

> It is impossible to exaggerate, and indeed difficult adequately to describe, the magnificence which now lies ahead ... One feels that one must be viewing the embankment of an abandoned main-line railway rather than a Roman road! (Margary, 1973.)

Johnston (1979) suggests that this was planned as a prestige road, but was little used, and proved to be a white elephant; indeed, one excavated section was found to have its metalling virtually intact. Hannigan (1994) describes the route from Old Sarum to Badbury Rings.

Blackstone Edge: an impressive section of the road from Manchester to Ilkley, which crosses the Pennines at a height of 1,475 feet (450m). It is a paved road which climbs straight up the hill above Littleborough at gradients of up to 1 in 4; the later packhorse track and two turnpike roads take much longer and less steep routes. This is one of only five places in Britain where a Roman road has a central line of stones; the curious feature here is that these stones have a deep groove, which is generally thought to have been created by the use of poles as brakes (Fig. 26). There has been much local controversy as to whether this is a Roman road at all!

25 *The massive agger of Ackling Dyke on Bottlebush Down, south-west of Salisbury, is one of the most impressive surviving Roman roads.*

26 *The paved Roman road crossing the Pennines at Blackstone Edge above Littleborough has a central groove, possibly used for braking.*

27 *Dere Street is overlain by the A68 for most of the 18 miles (29 km) north of Hadrian's Wall; there are numerous dire warnings to modern-day drivers.*

Dere Street: from York to Corbridge and across the Cheviots into Scotland; much is still in use south of Hadrian's Wall (notably the A1 to Scotch Corner). Beyond the Wall many sections are still very clear; here the directness of this road over the hilly country has made the A68 into a notoriously dangerous switchback (Fig. 27).

Devil's Causeway: a branch from Dere Street just north of the Wall, leading to Berwick; its name derives from a Dark Age superstition about its origins. Most of it is no longer used as a road, and little now remains.

Ermine Street: the main route from London via Godmanchester, Water Newton, Lincoln and the Humber estuary to York. It was laid out very skilfully at an early date, and has an overall directness similar to that of Watling Street and the Foss Way. Much of it is still a main road, notably many sections of the A1(M) north of London, but the section for 30 miles (48 km) from Colsterworth north along the chalk ridge to Lincoln is now either a B road or simply a track: it is known here as High Dyke, and was later used as a drove road (Fig. 28). The section north of Lincoln is a magnificent stretch of road, still in use for most of the way to the Humber (A15 and B1207). As a route to York this section was replaced by the Great North Road which leads off to the west only 3 miles (5 km) north of Lincoln, going via Doncaster and Tadcaster, thus avoiding the Humber crossing.

Peddars Way: From Ixworth to the Wash, where there was probably a ferry; it was the central part of the route from Colchester to Lincoln. It was a well-built road, but curiously runs parallel to the Icknield Way. It is now mostly a green lane or footpath, and has been designated as a long-distance path; the final 20-mile (32 km) length from Castle Acre to Holme next the Sea is an excellent walk (Robinson, 1986, Hannigan 1994).

28 *Ermine Street south of Lincoln was later used by generations of drovers. It became known as High Dyke, and was finally incorporated in the enclosed field system.*

Via Devana: Colchester to Ermine Street (Godmanchester); the name is eighteenth century, based on the suggestion that it was the route to Chester (Deva). It survives as a green lane for 11 miles (18 km) south-east of Cambridge; here it became known in the Middle Ages as Wool Street (originally Wolvestreet!).

THE END OF THE ROMAN ERA

Following the collapse of Roman rule around AD 400, the roads were no longer maintained and many of those with minimal engineering simply disappeared back into the landscape. The major roads survived, and many remained in use, even though the new settlers shunned them when choosing sites for their settlements. Even at the end of the Dark Ages, after 600 years of total neglect, they were clearly still usable; at worst they were the easiest way across the country. From medieval times onwards, those which remained in use were altered to a greater or lesser extent. Some became rutted or were turned into holloways by the sheer pressure of

traffic, while others were later improved as turnpike or enclosure roads. These improvements often obliterated what then remained of the original road, and more recently many have been regraded and covered with tarmac. Such changes will inevitably have destroyed much of the original structure of the Roman road, though later roads often diverted from the Roman line, either to pass through a village or town, or in order to take an easier gradient – here the old agger may still survive.

The importance of Roman roads in the growth of the road system of Britain is very great indeed, despite the fact that their roads and towns were imposed on the countryside, rather than growing from the demands of local people. Numerous Roman roads are still in use today, whether as main roads such as the A5, country lanes or simply as tracks or footpaths. There was to be no more large-scale road maintenance until 1555, and no more deliberate road construction until the improvement of the turnpikes in the early years of the 19th century.

Chapter Three
MEDIEVAL ROUTES

THE DARK AGES

After the departure of the Romans and the demise of their political and economic systems, Britain entered what is popularly called the Dark Ages, thus called because there is little historical evidence. There was certainly much less trade and travel, and thus less need for roads. As for the prehistoric period, it is difficult to be at all precise about roads in the Dark Ages, save that many Roman roads clearly remained in use.

The Saxons had arrived in substantial numbers by the sixth century, and it used to be thought that they introduced the village to the British landscape. In fact, most villages were not established until at least the eleventh century, and, until that date, most people lived only in individual farmsteads or in settlements no larger than hamlets. The northern and western parts of Britain never had villages imposed upon them, and the tracks and lanes which still run from one isolated farm or hamlet to the next may well have changed little over thousands of years.

Not enough is known about the overall pattern of Dark-Age settlement to be able to say very much about the tracks which were in use. It appears that the sites on which the Saxons (and later the Danes) chose to live were usually away from Roman roads, presumably on the grounds that those routes would only bring trouble. As we have already seen, it is stunningly clear throughout the English Midlands that Roman roads often form the boundaries of parishes, rather than going through the settlements at their centres. Their aggers and ditches provided clear and convenient dividing lines in the landscape.

Anglo-Saxon charters sometimes have clauses describing these boundaries, and thus may provide the earliest documentary evidence for roads (Hooke, 1977). Several words are commonly used: *Straet* usually refers to a Roman or paved road, whilst *paeth* and *weg* refer to tracks, the latter sometimes given more explicitly as *holanweg* (holloway; a road hollowed out by the passage of people and animals; Figs. 29 and 32). It is important to realise that the reference to a road as a boundary does not tell us whether the road was actually in use at the time.

The minor road system of Britain was created piecemeal over a very long period, simply through the needs of farmers to get to their fields and pasture, or to travel to neighbouring settlements. In some places the lanes may well be prehistoric in origin, elsewhere Roman, Saxon, Danish or medieval; certainly many rural tracks are of great antiquity. It is highly probable that the system of minor roads was essentially complete in terms of length by AD 1000, though it has continued to change its form ever since.

During the Dark Ages there were many warring factions, and from time to time certain routes were used by armies; these became known as 'herepaths' (army roads). A good example is the Salisbury Way, leading from Shaftesbury via White Sheet Hill and Chiselbury to Salisbury. Its origins are probably prehistoric, but it is mentioned as a herepath

29 *The deeply entrenched holloway climbing up to White Sheet Hill from Shaftesbury has probably been used since prehistoric times. Traffic now takes the A30 in the valley below.*

and boundary in two Anglo-Saxon charters, it was used as a drove road and eventually it became part of the main coach road to the west from Salisbury. It is now a quiet green lane (Figs. 29 and 30). The Wiltshire Herepath is another well-preserved track which runs from Marlborough to Avebury over Fyfield Down. It too may have prehistoric origins, as a branch of the Great Ridgeway (see Fig. 3); it was also used until the 18th century as a coach road.

For most of this period there were few functioning towns and little trading, and thus even the Roman roads would have seen hardly any traffic. Trade did eventually start to grow again, notably in the years around the start of the ninth century, and this led to the naming of certain tracks as Port Ways, each leading to a particular port or market town. These were usually prehistoric tracks or Roman roads being used again. Many continued to be called Port Ways during the medieval period. The *Anglo-Saxon Chronicle* mentions the Portway from Northampton to Southampton via Oxford, and a well-known example is the Roman road from Silchester to Old Sarum (Salisbury); it is no longer a through route, and its use near the abandoned Roman town of Silchester must have ceased early in Saxon times. In Derbyshire, a Portway has been traced from Nottingham to Wirksworth and Bakewell by a succession of documentary references and place-names (Dodd, 1980).

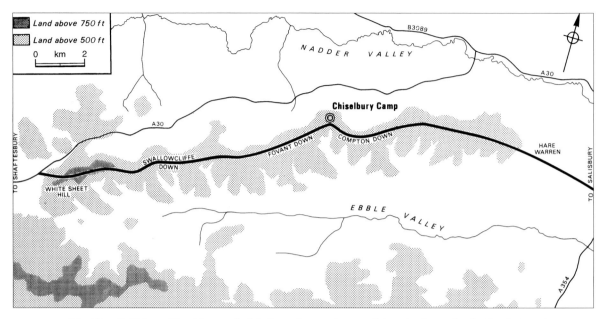

30 *The 'Salisbury Way' has probably been in use since prehistoric times. In the Dark Ages it was a herepath (army path), and later became a drove road and coach road.*

The Saxon struggle against the Danish invasion led to the creation of a network of fortified places (*būrhs*) by the early 10th century; the Danes also established boroughs. Many of these defended places, such as Wallingford, Shaftesbury, Wareham, Derby, Nottingham and Bedford attracted trade, and they mark the beginnings of medieval urban growth. They became important both as military and trading centres, and the old roads leading to them must have seen an increasing amount of traffic. The changes to the roads leading into Stamford, Winchester and Tamworth are outlined by Taylor (1979). At Stamford, the first Saxon settlement seems to have been away from the Roman road, almost half a mile downstream, near an easy fording point (Fig. 31). In the late ninth century the Danes built a fort close by, and when the area was reconquered by the English thirty years later, they built a new *būrh* on the opposite side of the river. The place where the main road crossed the river simply moved downstream in response to the changing settlement pattern.

MEDIEVAL MAIN ROADS

By the early 11th century political control had been steadily consolidated, and a single English kingdom had emerged. At the same time the medieval trading system was growing. Trade was inextricably linked with urban growth, because most trading was conducted in towns, immune from the new restrictions of feudalism. At the time of the Domesday Survey (1086) there were probably only about 50 places in England with genuine urban features and functions, yet by the early 14th century there were between five and six hundred towns, and most had grown considerably in size.

As a general rule, those towns which were located on major routes or at important junctions prospered, whilst others situated or deliberately planted even only a short distance from a road, often failed to grow. Examples of the failures include Church Brough (Cumbria), superseded by Market Brough on the main road less than half a mile away, and Beaudesert (Warwickshire) which was replaced by Henley in Arden, less than 200 yards (180m) distant.

Sometimes long-established roads were deliberately diverted or new bridges built so that traffic had to pass through a town's market place; this happened at St Ives (Cambridgeshire), Boroughbridge, Thame (Oxford) and Montacute (Somerset). At Ludlow the building of a new bridge across the Teme early in the 13th century achieved the same result. The study of streets within towns is a fascinating one, and takes in their layout, planning, width, status, diversions and names (Hindle, 1990).

Most towns also had access to rivers and the sea; it is important to remember that heavy or bulky goods were transported to, and then by, water wherever possible, even if our concern here is only with the roads.

The growth of towns has been well studied, but precisely how goods were moved from one place to another, and, more importantly, what routes were used and what was the nature of the resulting road network, are topics which have been given very little attention. This curious omission is almost certainly due to the paucity of the available evidence; relatively few direct records of such commonplace activities as travel and trade survive. It used to be thought that few people travelled beyond their own manor at this time, but this was clearly not the case. Most peasants would have travelled regularly to the local market or county town, and there were many other travellers such as workmen, minstrels, messengers, bishops, preachers and friars, pardoners, pilgrims, justices, taxmen and outlaws, quite apart from the all important merchants (Jusserand, 1889). The road system was a vital and integral part of the whole medieval economy, and, as such, deserves more study than it has so far received.

SOURCES

The sources for the study of medieval roads are varied. The remains of the roads and tracks themselves, whether seen from the ground or from aerial photographs, can be difficult to

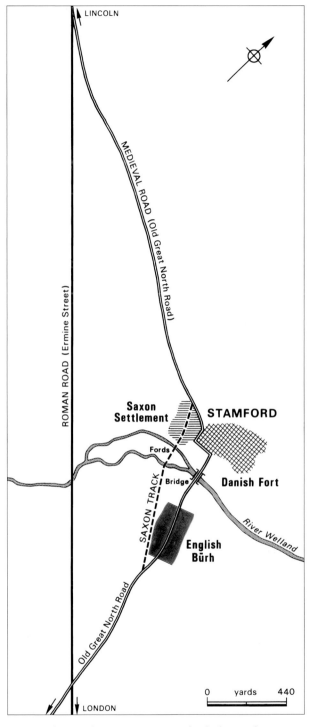

31 *The road pattern at Stamford changed during the Dark Ages in response to the changing settlement sites of the Saxons, Danes and then English. (After Taylor, 1979.)*

32 *The steep holloway running down from the deserted medieval village of Richard's Castle, south of Ludlow, now sees very little traffic.*

interpret; it is impossible by archaeological methods to date a road which has not been deliberately constructed, even if the remains are substantial. In physical terms, most medieval roads would have been packhorse tracks, though the major routes must have been capable of taking wagons. On slopes these often became sunken roads or 'holloways', because of the erosion caused by the traffic, made worse by the rain (Fig. 32). A common feature is the spreading out and duplication of tracks where a route left cultivated land, or where a hill had to be climbed. Many such rutted holloways are described as being medieval, but their origins may either lie far earlier, or even later.

The building and repairing of bridges was regarded as a pious act in medieval times, and is quite well recorded; special taxes (pontages) could also be levied. Sometimes a new bridge altered the whole pattern of traffic in an area, with consequences far away. For example, the building of Harnham Bridge south of the new town of Salisbury in 1244 diverted traffic from Wilton which had formerly been the major town in the area. Equally, the building of the bridge at Abingdon probably contributed to the decline of Dorchester on Thames and even Wallingford. The new 12th-century bridge over the Ure at Boroughbridge diverted the course of the Great North Road, so that it crossed the river half a mile upstream, at the new town.

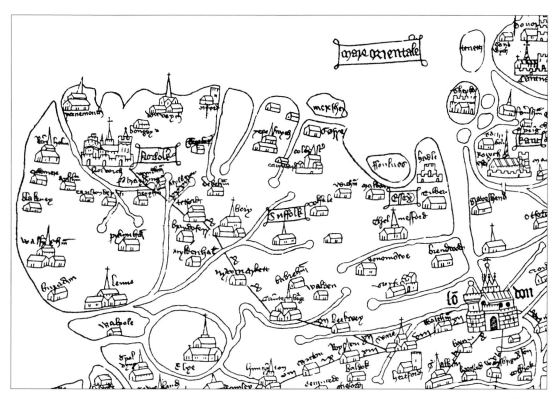

33 *East Anglia as shown on the Gough Map. The road from London to Norwich, plus part of the Great North Road are clearly shown, together with distances between the towns. The map is probably late 13th century; east is at the top.*

The old Roman road degenerated into a grassy lane, and finally ceased to be a road altogether when the area was enclosed in 1809.

Causeways were effectively extended bridges across marshes or wide rivers. Maud Heath's Causeway near Chippenham is one of the more substantial and unusual examples; it is 4½ miles (7 km) in length, and was built soon after 1474, enabling people to cross the river Avon dry-shod. The causeways across the Fens to Ely are probably medieval in origin, they were certainly being extensively maintained and improved at this time.

The best evidence for medieval roads comes from those documentary sources which show that someone actually travelled along a particular road. The itineraries of the medieval monarchs are the most detailed records, giving a day-to-day record of the movements of the king and of his household, from the time of King John onwards. These early monarchs were itinerant – John moved over 13 times a month on average throughout his reign, in both summer and winter. Thus we have an invaluable record, even if the kings travelled to some places which the ordinary traveller would not visit. Moving the paraphernalia of the royal household (including the chancery and exchequer) required up to twenty carts and wagons, and reasonable roads were clearly needed. There are also a few surviving records of the movement of goods; the best are those kept by the government when buying food to provision armies abroad. With bulky goods such as grain, it is clear that rivers were used wherever possible. Some monastic and estate records also give details of the movement of goods, but rarely of the precise routes taken.

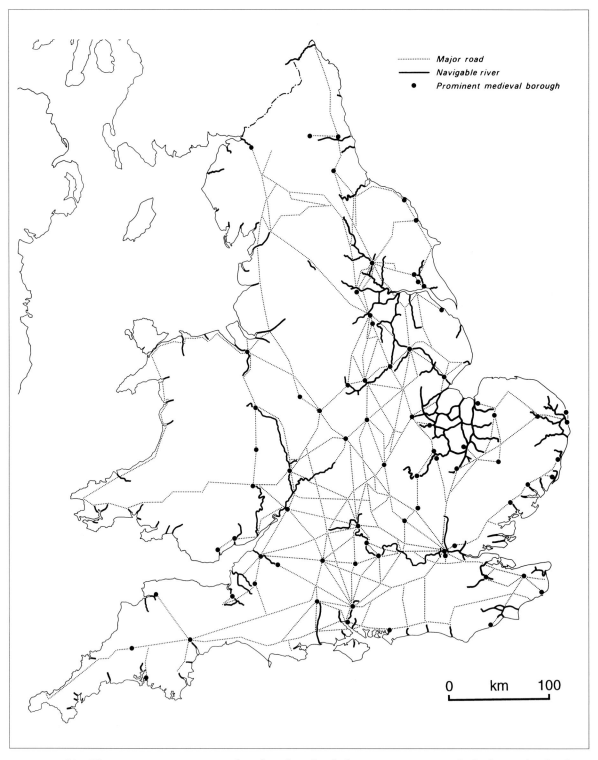

34 *The transportation system of medieval England; the major towns were linked to each other by both road and river.*

The number of documents, whether of local, legal, monastic or national origin, increases in the later medieval period; some can be used to identify stretches of road. A whole host of words in various languages are used to refer to roads: the Saxon *paeth*, *straet* and *weg* give way to the Latin *strata* and *via*, and the English gate and highway, among many others. There were also more complex descriptions such as *via regia*, *magna via*, or *stayngate* (stony road – usually a later description of a Roman road). A selection from Derbyshire includes *Viam Comitis* (the Earl's Way), Broad Gate, Castlegate, Peakway and Alsopeway (the way to Alsop). In Wales and the Welsh borders, road place-name elements include *ffordd*, *heol* and *sarn*. Road name evidence should not be relied on uncritically; for example, a road might have been given a name out of ignorance or superstition. A herepath may never have been trodden by an army, and a *via regia* may never have seen a king, though such a name implies a certain degree of importance for a road.

There are also a number of court cases concerning roads, such as that against the Abbot of Chertsey in 1386, who had allowed two 'wells' to exist in the high road from Egham to Staines. The Abbot was in court, not for failing to maintain the road, but because a hapless man had drowned in one of the holes, and the Abbot had claimed his goods! Elsewhere, men were prosecuted for ploughing up roads, planting hedges too close and even for erecting buildings on the highway. The wholly negative evidence given by such cases is probably not representative of the general condition of most roads. The fact that the kings and their entourage managed to travel throughout the year suggests that the roads were in a reasonable state.

There is a further important legal point: the medieval concept of a road was that it was a right of way, or an 'easement', rather than a physical entity. Thus if a section was foundrous or impassable, the traveller had the right to diverge from it, even to the extent of trampling crops. This may well be the root cause of some of the twists and turns in many country lanes which can still be seen today.

Perhaps the most important single source of information about the main roads is the Gough Map, probably first drawn in the late 13th century, and revised in about 1360, which shows a network of almost 3,000 miles (4,800 km) of roads in England and Wales (Fig. 33). London is clearly the centre of a network of roads radiating out to all parts of the kingdom. Even where roads are not shown, the towns *en route* are usually shown correctly. About 40 per cent of the routes shown are on the lines of Roman roads, whereas the rest were the new medieval roads which made and maintained themselves simply through the continual passage of traffic.

It is possible to make a number of general statements about the network of major roads in medieval times (Hindle, 1998c). First, many Roman roads remained in use, still providing the easiest way across the country. Second, new medieval roads came into being simply through habitual use. Third, the road system as a whole was adequate for the amount of traffic that existed, even in winter. Fourth, roads often acted as feeders to the river system for the movement of heavy or bulky merchandise. Finally, it is clear that many of today's major roads were created or used in the medieval period, simply because of the need to service the great growth of medieval agriculture, industry and trade. Of course, many routes simply reused earlier tracks. By the end of the medieval period there was a well-integrated transport network, well capable of serving the needs of the economy (Fig. 34).

Clearly, many of the types of road described in following chapters were in use in medieval times. Drove roads have their origins in this period as do many trading routes such as 'saltways'; trade routes became much more important later and are dealt with in chapters 5 and 6.

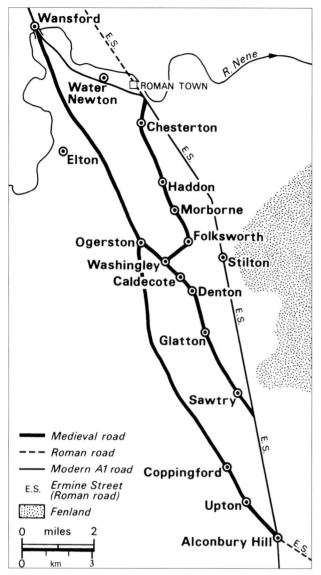

35 *Some medieval roads in Cambridgeshire.*
(After Taylor, 1979)

A few of the county studies in 'The Making of the English Landscape' series stress the importance of roads in the development of the medieval landscape; of particular note are those of Northamptonshire by Steane (1974) and of Hertfordshire by Munby (1977). An introduction to the evidence for medieval roads in Scotland is given in Fenton and Stell (1984).

LOCAL STUDIES

Local studies of medieval routes may look at major or minor roads; they may take a specific road, or try to reconstruct the road network of a particular area, whether a single parish, or a whole county. Examples can be found for Derbyshire in Dodd (1980), for the Yorkshire Dales in Wright (1985), for the Lake District in Hindle (1998a) and for Northamptonshire and elsewhere in Taylor (1979). All show how detailed historical study together with field observation can produce excellent results. Taylor gives an interesting example in Cambridgeshire, showing how the routes along the line of Ermine Street altered during the medieval period (Fig. 35). Here the Roman road seems to have been abandoned for drier routes to the west, notably through Coppingford and Ogerston, neither of which now survives as a village. This route is no longer a through route, as the A1 has largely reverted to the Roman line.

Many features in the landscape are not fixed, but are in a continual state of evolution and change. The local road network is no exception, evolving to serve the changing pattern of settlement, just as the major road network changed as towns grew and prospered. Virtually the only place where it is possible to find a guaranteed 'medieval road' (i.e. one which was not in existence before or used since) is where a road leads to the site of a village created and then deserted in the medieval period, or one leading to a failed medieval new town.

At the parish level there were numerous tracks leading from the farms and villages to fields, pasture and woodland, and it is all too easy to forget them in looking at the more important routes. Indeed, these tracks have rarely been studied in any detail. They can be glimpsed in early estate plans, for although the earliest of these were not drawn until the late 16th century, they may still show much of the medieval layout. A map of Padbury (Buckinghamshire), drawn in 1591 depicts numerous irregular tracks leaving the village, their main

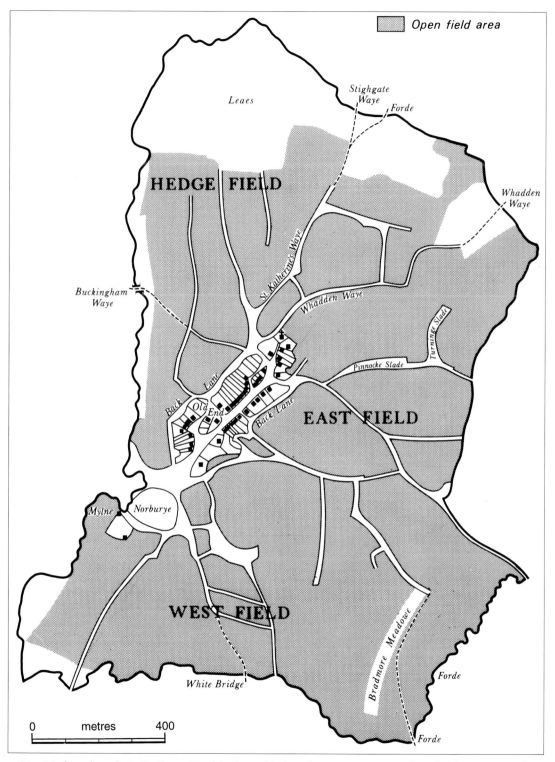

Open field area

Leaes

Stighgate Waye

Forde

HEDGE FIELD

Whadden Waye

St. Katherines Waye

Buckingham Waye

Whadden Waye

Turninge Slade

Pinnocke Slade

Back Lane

Old End

Back Lane

EAST FIELD

Mylne

Norburye

WEST FIELD

Bradmore Meadowe

Forde

White Bridge

Forde

0   metres   400

36 *Medieval tracks in Padbury (Buckinghamshire) as shown on an estate plan of 1591; most simply gave access to the fields and did not reach the parish boundary.*

function being to give access to the fields; many do not even reach the parish boundary (Fig. 36). Most such field tracks have been destroyed by later ploughing or by enclosure (see Chapter 8). However, where the ridge and furrow pattern of medieval fields still survives, the unploughed headlands which gave access and a turning place for the plough, and the holloways leading to the next village can often still be traced.

Even where the physical remains have been totally removed, there may be other map evidence in pre-enclosure or tithe maps, even though these may be as late as the mid-19th century in date, and thus somewhat remote from the medieval period (Hindle, 1998b). It should also be remembered that many field tracks go back much further than the medieval period, having their origins in Roman or prehistoric times.

In areas where arable cultivation was not the norm, fields and the tracks leading to them might be very irregular, both being created piecemeal as needed. Any upland area of western Britain such as the Lake District or Dartmoor has such tracks, and beyond the enclosed area, tracks lead out on to the moors. Each Lakeland village has its own section of fell, the two being connected by various tracks along which the sheep and cattle would be driven. Areas brought into cultivation from other types of waste land such as forest or fen also had their access routes. However, unless there is documentary evidence, it is difficult to date any of these tracks.

CHURCH PATHS
AND CORPSE ROADS

A few tracks were used principally for access to the parish church. Sometimes documentary evidence survives; in the accounts of the Bailiff of the Forest of Dartmoor for 1491, a parcel of land is described as bounded by a 'Churchway' to Widecombe (Hemery, 1986). In the extreme south-west of Cornwall (West Penwith) these ways have been identified as

'church paths', many of which are named as such in documents, often in the Cornish equivalent, *'forth eglos'* (usually shortened to *'freglos'*) (Maxwell, 1976). In medieval times, this area had only 13 parish churches, and church paths led to them from outlying farmsteads up to 3 miles (5 km) away. Many of the paths were marked by granite wayside crosses. Over a hundred of these crosses remain, though others have been lost and are represented only by field names.

Rather better known are the corpse roads which were used for taking the dead from isolated farms or hamlets to the parish church for burial. These roads were usually little more than packhorse tracks, as most coffins would have been carried on horseback. They are best seen in the more remote areas of the country where the parishes are large and most farmsteads lie far from the church. The different names for such roads around the country include coffin roads, kirk roads and lich or lych ways (lich is an old word for a corpse). There is often little documentary evidence of their use; indeed it may be nothing more than local tradition.

Robertson (1947) describes several such tracks in the Highlands of Scotland, including routes from Glen Strath Farrar to Kintail, from Quoich Bridge to Glen Shiel, and from Glen Garry to Glen Moriston. Less than 10 miles (16 km) south of Edinburgh, a 'kirk road' runs from Bavelaw and Loganlee across the pass between Carnethy and Scald Law (the highest point of the Pentland Hills) to the church at Penicuik.

Examples in northern England include a corpse road which runs from Garrigill (in the South Tyne valley above Alston) for 11 miles (18 km), reaching a height of almost 2,600 ft (800m) on Cross Fell, before descending to the mother church at Kirkland in the Eden valley. Only a few miles to the south there is a parallel route from Birkdale in Upper Teesdale, which runs for 12 miles (20 km), passing through the great gash of High Cup to the parish church at

37 *The villagers of Mardale Green carried their dead for burial on this track over the fells to Shap until 1736. The remains of the village are normally submerged beneath Haweswater.*

Dufton. The track through the chasm is known as Narrowgate; the whole route is still in use as part of the Pennine Way. Further south, in Swaledale, bodies were carried in wicker baskets from the area around Keld at the top of the dale, for over 12 miles (20 km) to the church at Grinton, until a burial ground was provided at Muker in 1580. In Derbyshire, the dead from Edale were taken over Hollins Cross for burial in Castleton until 1633.

The Lake District also has several corpse roads; one led from the village of Mardale Green (now usually submerged beneath Haweswater) to the mother church at Shap, some 7 miles (11 km) distant (Fig. 37). Leaving the village it climbs steeply via a series of zigzags on to Mardale Common, reaching 1,656 ft (500m), it then descends into the little visited valley of Swindale, and finally crosses the moor to the church where it is known as the Kirk Gate (i.e. Church Road). The chapel at Mardale was granted its own burial ground in 1728, and the last corpse was taken to Shap in 1736. Another Lakeland example is the remote track across Burnmoor, which connects the tiny hamlet of Wasdale Head with St Catherine's church at Boot, over 6 miles (10 km) away.

Much the same conditions led to the creation of a Lich Way across Dartmoor, as all those who died within the area of the ancient Forest of Dartmoor had be buried at Lydford until 1260. The people worst affected were those who lived in the centre of the moor, only a few miles from the church at Widecombe. Instead, they had to take corpses across the moor, climbing to a height of over 1,500 ft (460m). Here weather conditions could be so bad that the direct route to Lydford could not be used, and roundabout routes had to be taken instead, which were often twice as long. There are several possible routes across the moor from Two Bridges, Bellever and Postbridge; they traverse the southern slopes of Cut Hill, and cross the Tavy near Wapsworthy, 3 miles (5 km) short of Lydford (Toulson, 1984; Hemery, 1986).

PILGRIM ROUTES

In a more pious age than our own, it was common for people to travel to visit the various shrines dotted around the country, as well as those abroad. In England, the shrine of St Swithun at Winchester was much visited, and pilgrims also travelled to remote places such as Hereford to seek a particular saint's aid. Ten different routes, of varying historical credence, are given by Sugden (1991).

The principal pilgrim destinations were the eleventh century chapel of Our Lady of Walsingham, and later the shrine of Thomas à Becket in Canterbury, set up after his murder in 1170.

At the start of *The Canterbury Tales*, written in about 1400, Chaucer says that once April comes,

> Thanne longen folk to goon on pilgrimages …
> And specially from every shires ende
> Of Engelond to Caunterbury they wende

His pilgrims travelled from Southwark, and only five places *en route* are mentioned (Depeford, Grenewych, Sidyngborne, Boghtoun under Blee and Bobbe-up-and-doun; the last is Harbledown). Although Chaucer uses the pilgrimage to string together a set of tales, he takes it for granted that his readers know the road, and he never mentions any difficulties of travel. We may assume that this Roman road was probably still in a reasonable state of repair. This was surely the most important single pilgrim route in later medieval England; the road was equally important as part of the main road to Dover and thence to France.

One particular route has become known as the 'Pilgrims' Way' (Jennett, 1971). It runs along the North Downs, beginning at Winchester, and proceeds via Alton to Farnham, along the Hog's Back past Guildford, then to Dorking, Titsey, Wrotham, Snodland, Charing and finally to Canterbury. In fact this is probably a route of much greater antiquity, its use long pre-dating the coming of pilgrims.

Hilaire Belloc (1910) called it the Old Road, and it is a typical ridgeway route (see Chapter 1). It may well have provided a route to and from the great ceremonial centres of Salisbury Plain. The original route from Stonehenge passed where Andover and Basingstoke now stand, and joined the Pilgrims' Way at Farnham; this older route is known as the Harrow Way (see Fig. 2). Several Roman villas appear to be connected with the Pilgrims' Way, though there is no evidence of the route being improved by the Romans.

Unfortunately, there is no real evidence for the use of this route by medieval pilgrims and the first mention of this romantic idea dates from the 18th century. In any case, the traffic of pilgrims lasted for less than four hundred years, and the track probably has its origins some three and a half thousand years ago. No doubt some pilgrims did use it, but its main users would have been drovers and traders, especially in the 18th century when they were trying to avoid the tolls of the newly turnpiked roads. It is always dubious to name a track after one particular type of user; only rarely was any road used for a single purpose.

Nevertheless, the passage of men and animals over thousands of years has created a very clear series of tracks and holloways along this route. Sometimes the route runs on top of the ridge, but more frequently it appears as a terrace on the scarp slope, as parts of the chalk ridge are topped with clay-with-flints which would have been hard going in wet conditions. Some sections are overlain by modern roads, whilst others remain as tracks or paths. It has been an important through-route for thousands of years, and the 'Old Road' is certainly a better name for it. More recently, the North Downs Way has been established as one of the many long-distance footpaths; its route has been chosen to avoid motor roads as much as possible, and only coincides in places with the various lines of the Old Road or the Pilgrims' Way (Herbstein, 1982).

MONASTIC ROUTES

There are many tracks with monastic connections which may appear at first sight to have a medieval origin. One such is the so-called Abbots' Way across southern Dartmoor which appears to connect Buckfast Abbey with the abbeys at Tavistock and Buckland. However, the track is certainly older than the abbeys, and although the monks no doubt used it, it was always known as the Jobbers' Path or Cawse until a traveller called John Andrews first dubbed it the Abbots' Way in 1794. In fact a parallel route some miles further north across the moor, which is marked with 22 stone crosses, appears to be a much better candidate as a monastic route. However, there is no direct evidence of monks using this track either (Peel, 1971; Groves, 1972; Toulson, 1983; Hemery, 1986; Hannigan, 1994).

Rather more successful has been the detailed investigation of the numerous routes connected with Strata Florida Abbey in Cardiganshire by Colyer (1984). The Welsh place-names include an abbey road, pilgrims' ford and monk's way; the study used detailed field observation and historical research.

In the Yorkshire Dales one of the most famous surviving monastic roads is Mastiles Lane, which was originally known as Strete Gate. It runs from Kilnsey (a grange or farm of Fountains Abbey) westwards across Malham Moor, heading for Ribblesdale and Clapham, and eventually for the Abbey's distant estates in the Lake District. Rights of passage were granted to the abbey's men, animals and goods throughout its length. Originally it was an unwalled track across the open moors, marked by crosses at prominent points; several of their bases are still in place. Mastiles Lane continued to be used by the drovers, driving their cattle from Scotland (see Chapter 5). When the whole area was eventually enclosed in the late 18th and early 19th centuries, it and numerous other drovers' routes were constrained between new walls which were

38 *The monastic route of Mastiles Lane in winter, crossing Malham Moor at a height of almost 1300 feet (400 m).*

built sufficiently far apart to allow easy passage for the herds of cattle. It is now one of the many 'green lanes' of the Pennines (Fig. 38).

The high medieval period was brought to a sudden end by the arrival of the Black Death in 1348, which cut the population by 40 per cent. Some villages began to be deserted as a result of the fall in population, and their roads went out of use. Plague became endemic, and for almost a century and a half, the economy barely prospered, a situation exacerbated by the Wars of the Roses. The amount of trade and traffic fell significantly, and once again there is little record of the road system; it almost certainly failed to grow until political and economic conditions improved in the 16th century.

Chapter Four

EARLY MODERN ROADS

WITH THE RE-ESTABLISHMENT of firm central government by Henry VII in 1485, there began a period of sustained economic growth, which has lasted, with only a few minor setbacks, until the present day. This chapter is essentially concerned with roads in the 16th and 17th centuries.

The monasteries had undertaken some maintenance of bridges and roads throughout the medieval period, and travellers rarely complained about the roads. John Leland was the first traveller to write about his travels. Around 1540 he visited most of the monasteries and makes frequent reference to bridges and river crossings, but says little about the roads, implying that most were in a reasonable condition. The dissolution of the monasteries in the late 1530s was one of Henry VIII's more drastic actions, and it may well be that the removal of the limited road repair undertaken by the monasteries, plus the growing amount of traffic, began to put strains on the road system. Another factor was that the climate was changing from the drier and warmer conditions of the medieval period towards the so-called 'Little Ice Age' with its wetter and cooler summers and colder winters. This too must have contributed to the rapid deterioration of the roads which became evident in the late 16th century.

The surviving sections of the Roman road system still formed the backbone of the main road system, but during the medieval period many local roads had also become part of this system, and were particularly vulnerable to the damage caused by the ever increasing traffic. During the reign of Elizabeth I, the fine balance between the amount of traffic and the roads' ability to maintain themselves was evidently broken. Soon, references to poor and impassable roads, and to the difficulty of travelling in winter, became progressively more frequent (Crofts, 1967). In 1586, William Harrison complained that some highways

> within these five and twentie yeares have beene in most places fiftie foot broad according to the law, whereby the traveller might ... passe by the loaden cart without danger of himself and his horsse; now they are brought unto twelve, or twentie, or six and twentie at the most.

Moreover, travel in winter in some areas was a particular problem:

> in the claie or cledgie soile they are often verie deepe and troublesome in the winter halfe.

Such comments were echoed by Camden, Speed, Pepys, Thoresby and Fiennes, among many others, during the 17th century. In the *Pilgrim's Progress* Bunyan uses the poor condition of so many roads as the model for the Slough of Despond.

The deterioration of the roads meant that the first English road legislation had to be passed in 1555, requiring each parish to repair all its own roads. Under earlier Common Law, a parish could be indicted for failing to repair its roads, but the new act was designed to promote regular road maintenance throughout the country. Parishioners were obliged to spend four days a year working on the roads, supervised by two surveyors appointed by the parish. As early as 1563 this was increased to six days, the surveyors were given stronger powers and the Justices were allowed to fine parishes which failed to maintain their roads. The statute was amended again in 1575 to allow the Justices to levy rates in order to repair particular roads. This was the beginning of a long series of Acts of Parliament concerning roads. For example, in 1691 minimum widths were laid down; 8 feet (2.4m) for roads to market towns, and 3 feet (1m) for horse causeys. From 1697 signposts could be required to be erected. This legislative process eventually culminated in the 18th-century turnpike acts (see Chapter 7). It was not until the General Highway Act of 1835 that the 1555 Act was repealed.

In theory, the parish repair system was a reasonable solution to the problem, so long as there was little long distance through traffic, but in practice it did not work well. There were many weaknesses in the system; the surveyors were essentially conscripted amateurs who were forced to do the job and to supervise unwilling labourers, many of whom never used the roads and thus had no interest in doing good work. Eventually, the six days of statute labour began to look like a holiday. The surveyors were appointed for only one year, were not paid, yet could be fined for negligence. There were a few keen exceptions, such as Benjamin Browne, sometime High Constable of Kendal, who undertook two surveys of his local roads in 1730-1. He had nothing good to say about any of them; most were described as narrow, bad and covered with hedges.

To make matters worse, some parishes had much more road to repair than others, some had a busy main road to maintain, whilst others had a small population unable to cope. But even if the full amount of labour was obtained, the known repair methods were very rudimentary, usually consisting of little more than applying gravel to the surface, or digging ditches:

> The nub of the matter was simply drainage. The worst roads suffered by virtue of the subsoil, by lack of any camber, by excessive gradients, by flooding, and by becoming so deeply rutted and pot-holed that the slightest deterioration in the weather made them into a morass. (Dyos & Aldcroft, 1969.)

It is hardly surprising that road repair by statute labour produced poor results. Essentially the problem was whether road users, local communities or the country as a whole should pay for the upkeep of roads. In fact, the successful improvement of road surfaces had to wait until the early 19th century and introduction of the techniques of McAdam, which were to be applied first to the turnpikes (see Chapter 7).

Until then the net result was that roads were often in an appalling state. This might be expected in the wetter and hillier areas of the north and west, but roads near London were often just as bad, notably those across the Wealden clays. Late in the 18th century Horace Walpole wrote to a friend:

> If you love good roads … be so kind as never to go into Sussex … Coaches grow there no more than balm or spices.

If the roads could not be adequately maintained, then the other way to improve matters was to try to restrict the carts, and especially the new wagons that were first mentioned in 1564. These became increasingly numerous on the roads from the late 16th century and were soon joined by private coaches, and then by stage-coaches in the first half of the next century. As early as 1621, Parliament tried to control the maximum weight of vehicles, especially in winter, or to restrict the number of horses, all to no avail. Once the roads had become deeply rutted, narrow wheels travelled best, but Parliament also tried from time to time to insist on broad wheels which it was thought would not only do less damage to the roads, but might also actually help to improve them. However, many wainwrights made matters worse by adding cogs to their narrow-rimmed wheels, which cut up the road surface even more, making it difficult for any other type of traffic to pass.

By 1660 there were regular coach services from London to the south-west, Lancashire, Newcastle and Edinburgh, and by 1705 some 180 towns had stage-coach services. Away from the main routes, however, the adoption of wagons and coaches spread only slowly from the area immediately around London. Beyond south-eastern England, wheeled traffic was rare, and most goods were moved by packhorse (Crofts, 1967). For example, Ralegh wrote in 1593 that it was impossible to take ordnance by land to Plymouth, whilst as late as 1749, a traveller observed that there was not one cart in the whole of Northumberland. The Weald had particular problems due to its heavy clays; an 18th-century gun founder had dragged 20 nine-foot-long nine-pounders to Lewes; he reported that they had:

> torn the roads so that nothing can follow them and the [people of the] country curse us heartily.

Even Manchester and Liverpool were linked to each other only by packhorse routes until 1760. Thus narrow packhorse tracks were the norm throughout most of Britain; these 'pack and prime ways' were obviously cheaper to maintain than a full-width wagon or cart road. It comes as something of a surprise to realise that most parts of Britain did not have roads fit for wheeled vehicles until the late 18th century. Another problem was that travellers and carriers also had to contend with robbers and highwaymen, not only in remoter areas, but also around London where rich pickings were to be had.

The postal system has its origins in the reign of Henry VIII and the first Postmaster-General was appointed by Elizabeth I; all official letters and parcels were carried by horse, and at first they were all routed through London

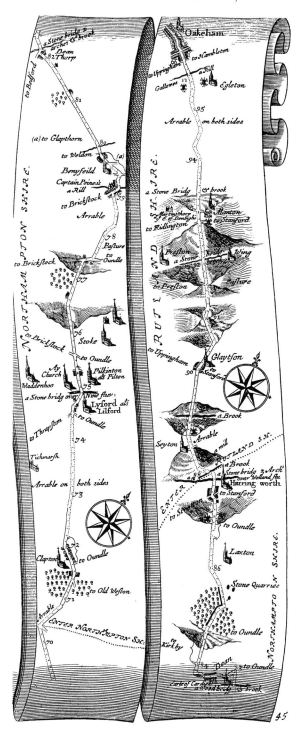

39 *An extract from a page of Ogilby's Britannia (1675) showing the road from Clapton to Oakham, plus numerous side roads and much other detail for the traveller.*

(Crofts, 1967). Non-official items had to be sent with drovers or carriers, whether by packhorse, cart or wagon. The important Holyhead mail route, allowing communication with Ireland, was well established by 1600; it used the route along the coast of North Wales. The Milford Haven post route was established soon after, it went by way of Cardiff, Swansea and Haverfordwest. The official postal service began to carry private mail from 1635. In 1663, letters from London to Derby took three days, but by 1711, the same time allowed letters to reach Edinburgh, at a cost of 6d. (2½p). Various cross-country routes were added during the 17th century, so that a comprehensive system of 'post-roads' emerged, together with Stage Towns and Branch Posts. There was nothing which made the post roads special other than the fact that mails were routinely carried along them. They are, however, an indication of the steadily growing economy and the need for good communications.

OGILBY AND FIENNES

The 17th century provides the first detailed cartographic evidence for roads on a national scale. The earliest county maps, produced by Saxton (1570s) and Speed (1612), did not show roads, but a list of the principal highways was given by William Harrison in his *Description of Britain* in 1586. However, almost a century later, the road maps in John Ogilby's *Britannia* (1675) illustrated the country

> By a Geographical and Historical DESCRIPTION of the Principal Roads thereof, Actually Admeasured and Delineated in a Century of Whole-Sheet *Copper-Sculps*.

Two hundred pages of text were interleaved with the hundred road maps, based on surveys carried out over the previous six years. It was a pioneering work, and it was to be over a century before it was superseded (Hindle, 1998b). Ogilby's road maps are an invaluable source, giving great detail of the main roads as well as indicating many minor roads.

Ogilby depicted each route in a series of scrolls, working across each page from bottom left to top right (Fig. 39). The roads are shown by solid lines where enclosed, and by dotted lines where they cross open country; down the centre of the roads are dots marking each quarter-mile or furlong, and the running mileage is also indicated. Numerous features on or near the roads such as bridges, rivers, castles, woods and churches are shown, all intended to help the traveller on his way. Steep hills are shown pictorially, with a hill indicating an ascent, and an upside-down hill a descent. These strip maps use a scale of one inch to the mile and thereby helped popularise the statute mile (it had been defined in 1593, though customary miles continued in use in many parts of the country for many years).

The road system depicted by Ogilby is substantial; it owes much to the roads built by the Romans some one and a half thousand years before. He shows a network which consists of eleven main roads leading from London to the provinces, linked by many cross-roads. Alternative routes are also given (some are described as 'worst' ways), and many side routes are indicated (Fig. 40). Ogilby's work was much copied, both in strip form and by adding his roads to county maps; this latter process began almost immediately, but the first complete set of county maps showing roads was not produced until 1695 by Morden. Ogilby's work became progressively out of date as the turnpikes were established; it was eventually replaced by a new survey, published as Cary's *New Itinerary* in 1798, again much copied by contemporary cartographers.

The most detailed records of travel in the years around 1700 are those left by Celia Fiennes, an early 'curious traveller' who travelled widely on horseback throughout England (Fiennes, 1982) (Fig. 41). The writings of this early tourist illustrate graphically the

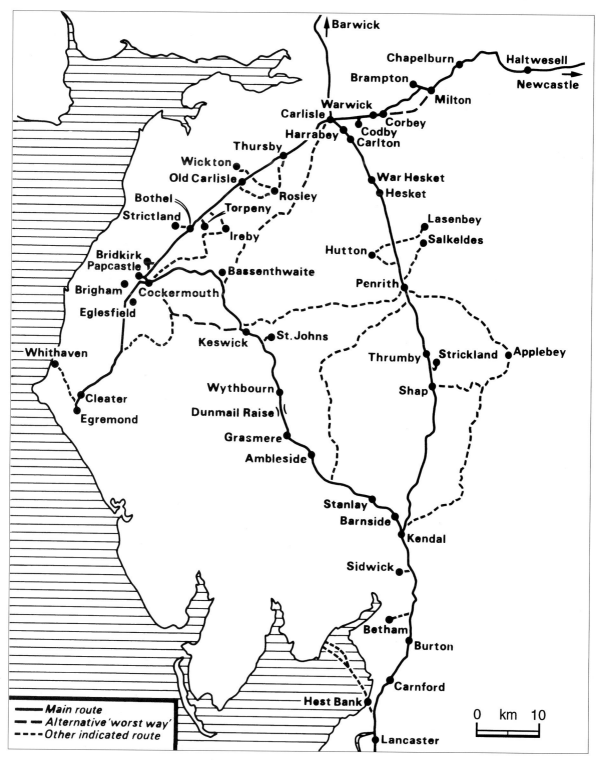

40 *The network of roads in Cumbria shown in Ogilby's road book is far greater than the four main routes which are given in detail.*

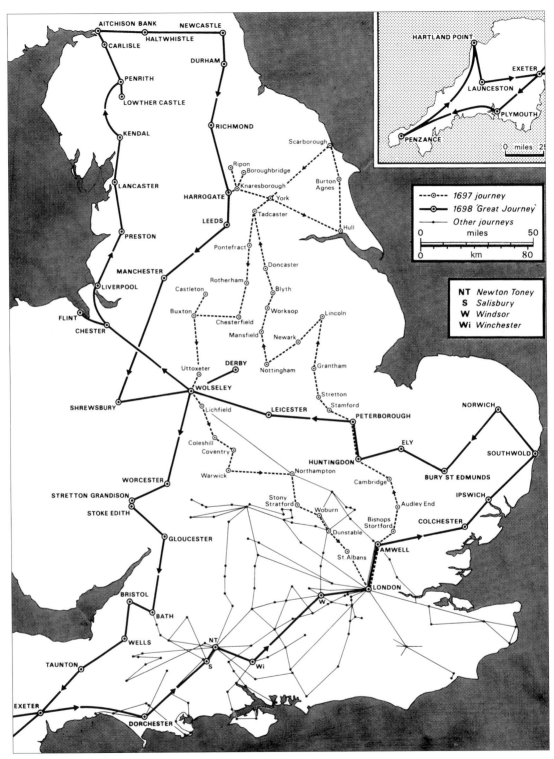

41 *The routes travelled by Celia Fiennes; this curious traveller visited most parts of England, and wrote much about the roads on which she travelled.*

poor state of the roads on the very eve of the turnpike mania. Most of her references to the roads are not complimentary. Towards Plymouth she reported that

> the wayes now became so difficult that one could scarcely pass by each other, even the single horses.

Travelling to Ely, the ways were

> very deep its mostly lanes and low moorish ground ... on each side deffended by the fendiks [fen dykes] ... and so you pass a flatt on a gravel Causey ... In the winter this Causey is over flowed.

Near Bath there was a

> narrow Causy that a Coach can scarce pass, all pitched with slatts and stones ... its made only for Packhorses ... the wayes to Bath are all difficult ... its steep ascents all ways out of the town.

As we have already seen, the Sussex roads were notorious; the road from Tunbridge to London via Sevenoaks was described as 'a sad deep clay way after wett'. Occasionally she reports good roads, sometimes going through parks on private roads, as at Leighton Hall north of Lancaster:

> had the advantage of going through parke and saved the going round a bad stony passage ... on to the road againe much of which was stony and steep, far worse than the Peake in Darbyshire.

She describes the strings of packhorses which were still much commoner on the roads than wagons, especially away from London: 'abundance of horses I see all about Kendall strectes with their burdens'. She notes that many roads could not take wheeled vehicles at all:

> The reason is plaine, from the narrowness of the lanes where is good lands ... and where its hilly and stoney no other carriages can pass.

This last description is of the road from Kendal to Windermere, which she says was capable of taking only narrow horse carts like wheel-barrows. Carriages simply could not travel along this road which appears on Ogilby's strip maps to be an important through route.

Finally she encountered the basic problems such as obtaining food and lodging, looking after her horses, and even finding the correct route:

> if you take a wrong Way there is no passing – you are forced to have Guides as in all parts of Darbyshire.

This was also true of many other parts of northern England, despite the fact that a law ordaining that signposts be erected had been passed in 1697.

In their different ways, Ogilby and Fiennes sum up the situation on the roads at the end of the 17th century. On the one hand there was a network of roads covering the country, on which an increasing number of carriers was operating; but on the other, many lengths of road were narrow, steep or poorly maintained. Packhorses remained the commonest means of transport, simply because wagons and coaches could not pass along most of the roads. The situation was, however, beginning to change, simply because trade was continuing to grow, and road improvements were being made; the first few turnpikes had already been enacted, and, as we have seen, one of the 1690s Highways Acts laid down minimum widths for different types of road.

Before turning to look in detail at the turnpikes, which marked such a fundamental change in the history of British roads, several special types of roads need some attention. The next two chapters will therefore deal with drove roads, packhorse tracks, and various unusual roads.

Chapter Five
DROVE ROADS AND PACKHORSE TRACKS

DROVE ROADS

The droving of cattle and sheep goes back into antiquity, probably starting with the transhumance movement of cattle and sheep between upland and lowland pastures. But from medieval times onwards, the long-distance droving trade grew steadily, reaching its

zenith in the early 19th century (Bonser, 1970; Toulson, 1980). In general, animals were driven from the northern and western areas of Britain to the growing towns of England. Cattle were driven from Scotland and Wales, most sheep came from Wales, though animals came from many other parts of the country too. Often the animals were kept for several months to be fattened at places along the drove roads where there was good grazing.

As with all migrations, the routes which were taken became standardised; not only out of habit and to take advantage of known facilities *en route*, but also because of the constraints of other features in the landscape. In hilly areas, there are obvious controls on the routes the cattle could take, but in the lowlands their routes were also constrained by the growing population and the ever-increasing number of enclosed fields. Sometimes these new fields encroached on traditional drove roads, and the drovers were often forced to keep to higher ground. They disliked travelling along newly walled, hedged or fenced roads through enclosed land, as there was little wayside forage for the cattle.

Drove roads are sometimes referred to as driftways, a 'drift' simply being another word for a 'drive' or 'drove'. Today they are also often

called 'green roads', though this term can include almost any old track now not covered by tarmac.

The height of the droving trade corresponded with the establishment of the turnpikes, which in some cases took over and improved roads which had long been used for droving. Many of the drovers used these improved roads, as they made rapid and efficient movement possible, even though other users of the turnpikes might be held up. On the other hand, drovers who wished to avoid the toll charges (which could amount to a substantial sum, given the frequency of toll bars and the long distances over which animals were driven) had to find new routes, or ways around the tollgates. As a result, some later drove roads took very peculiar and difficult routes and many drove roads had a network largely independent of the turnpikes.

Drove roads were formerly very numerous, though now their physical remains tend to be rather fragmentary, giving little idea of the original network, especially in lowland England. They can appear in very different forms. They may be wide swathes across open hill or moorland where there was little to stop the animals choosing their own course, or narrow sunken roads (holloways) where there was a steep slope or some other constriction, or wide enclosed lanes running through farmland. Modern highways now overlie some drove roads, but many others survive as country lanes. Yet others have been lost through disuse, or destroyed by recent afforestation. Most drove roads were punctuated by overnight grazing grounds (stances or halts);

42 *Cattle were formerly driven south along this section of Galwaithegate, until the railway over Shap was completed in 1846; the M6 (to the left) now carries most of the traffic.*

they were typically 8 to 12 miles (12 to 20 km) apart, and often had an inn. Of course these roads were not used solely by drovers, but by a great variety of other travellers too.

Drove roads can be traced in a variety of ways; there are the physical remains of the tracks, written records, descriptions written by contemporary travellers, and maps or road books naming certain roads as droves. Inn, farm, road and place names can give useful clues: field names such as Half Penny Field may relate to overnight stopping places, and inn names along drove roads include *Drover's Rest, Black Bull, White Ox* or *Brown Cow*. In England, the inn names may refer to the origins of the droves, such as *Scotch Inn, Welsh Arms* or *Craven Heifer* with more unusual examples

including *Tam O'Shanter, Highland Laddie* and *Caledonian*. Because many inns have ceased to trade and others changed their names since droving ended, it is useful to check lists of inns in early 19th-century directories. The antiquity of droving is well demonstrated by the road name *Galwaithegate* (the Galloway Road) given to a road south of Tebay (Westmorland) in a late 12th-century charter (Fig. 42). Not far away there is also a track still marked on the OS map as Galloway Gate going south from the Eden valley towards Ribblehead (Fig. 43).

SCOTTISH DROVE ROADS
This network extended from the Highlands and Islands with a multitude of tracks leading

43 *This former drove road climbs out out the Eden valley above Garsdale Head; it is still known as Galloway Gate. In the heyday of droving there were no walls and probably no precisely defined track.*

across the hills, aiming for various local cattle markets. There were essentially two main streams: one from the west coast and Skye, and the other from the far north. In the early days, these streams converged on Crieff, where the most important cattle fair or Tryst was held in the early autumn each year; after 1770 it was transferred to Falkirk. At these Trysts many of the cattle were bought by English dealers, and then driven southwards. Defoe, writing in 1726, noted that some cattle were driven all the way from Caithness to East Anglia, a distance of around 600 miles (965 km). Most glens in the Highlands saw the passage of large herds of cattle at some time; though the routes in use at any particular date can be difficult to ascertain (Fig. 44) (Haldane, 1973; Moir, 1975). Moreover, many areas were not farmed and

thus not enclosed, and so the drove roads would not have been precisely defined; rather the drovers and their cattle would have taken whatever route seemed easiest, just as had been the case with the prehistoric trackways (see Chapter 2).

The Highlands and Islands were suited for little else but the rearing of cattle, and those areas close to the sea with milder climates were especially favoured, even though they were extremely remote from the markets. There were numerous local collecting centres where cattle were gathered together. Cattle from the outer islands were taken to Skye, and then forced to swim across to the mainland at Kyle Rhea, near Glenelg (Fig. 45). There was a choice of routes onward; the first was over the Ratagan pass to Glen Shiel and the Great Glen and then

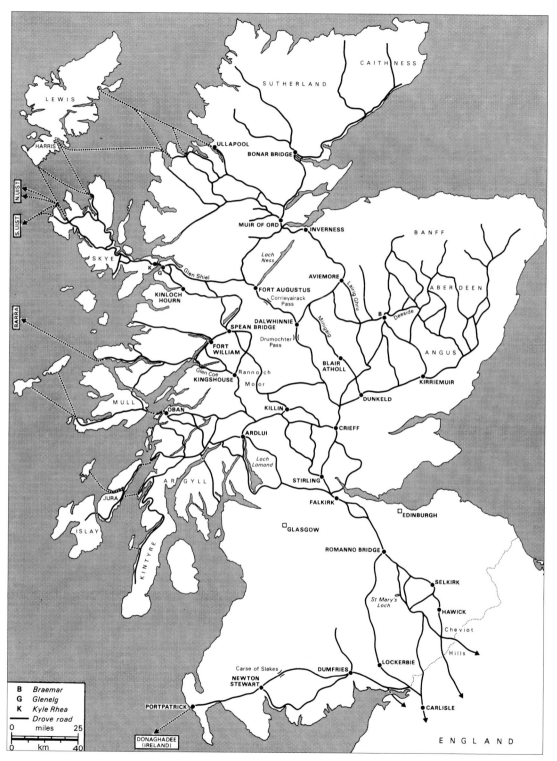

44 *The complex network of Scots drove roads led from far north and west of the country, heading for the Trysts at Crieff and then Falkirk. (After Haldane, 1973.)*

45 *Cattle gathered from the Hebrides swam across from Skye to the mainland at Kyle Rhea, near Glenelg, before starting the long drove south to the markets in England.*

over the high Corrieyairack Pass to Crieff, a route which was to be one of the first military roads (see Chapter 6). Another route from Kyle Rhea lay further south, via Kinloch Hourn and Glen Garry to Spean Bridge, a route which Telford proposed making into a road in 1811 (see Chapter 7). From here, there were three possible routes, and most cattle met again at the head of Glencoe before crossing Rannoch Moor (Fig. 46). There were many other routes from Skye and the west coast, for example from Arisaig, Mull, Argyll, Islay and Kintyre.

The story is similarly complex for the cattle from the rest of Scotland. The main routes from the north converged on Muir of Ord, and then divided again, one way going via Inverness and Aviemore, the other via Fort Augustus and over the Correyairack Pass. The latter was evidently preferred, even though it was a harder route, possibly because the drovers chose to be further away from civilisation, but certainly because abundant grazing was available. The two routes met again to cross the Drumochter Pass, now followed by the railway and the much improved A9 (Fig. 47). To the east are two long-disused tracks from Speyside to Blair Atholl; the older is Comyn's Road which was built in the thirteenth century, and was later known as the Way of the Waggon Wheels. It was replaced by the Minigaig Pass even further east in the 16th century. Both routes were shorter than

46 *This is the Old Glencoe Road (the Military Road as improved by Telford). This drove road sign near Victoria Bridge, south of the Black Mount, is incorrect; the drovers usually went along the other shore of Loch Tulla (see Fig. 71).*

Drumochter, but both climbed to over 2,600 feet (790m) (Kerr, 1991; Storer, 1991). They were replaced by the military road over Drumochter in 1729. Many other Highland drove routes were followed by the 18th-century military roads (see Chapter 6), whilst others were improved in the early 19th century by Telford, who was much concerned to help the droving trade (see Chapter 7).

Moray, Aberdeen and Angus had their own rather less rugged routes to the Trysts, long before this part of Scotland became famous for cattle breeding. In these lower coastal areas, many old drove roads have disappeared beneath later roads, been compressed between walls, or been obliterated by enclosure or new fields.

South of Falkirk, several routes led over the hills towards England. The routes spread out as there was no immediate common goal, and there are several relatively easy alternative routes. Many cattle seem to have been driven across the Pentland Hills via Cauldstane Slap to Romanno Bridge. One route then went down the Annan valley to Lockerbie and Carlisle, whilst others went via Selkirk and Hawick either to Teviothead, Langholm and Carlisle or into the Tyne valley along the Roman Dere Street, heading for the Great North Road and eastern England. Hannigan (1994) describes a drove road from Peebles to Ettrick. Many early maps of this area depict drove roads across the southern uplands and the Cheviots. Much of

47 *The Drumochter Pass is now traversed by the A9, leaving little trace of the drovers who once passed this way from the north of Scotland towards the Trysts.*

this area was devoid of settlement and agriculture, and presented few obstructions to the drovers.

Galloway also produced cattle for the droving trade, and in addition animals were brought across from Ireland to Portpatrick. All these cattle were driven eastwards to Dumfries, and then either joined the Scots cattle at Carlisle, or were driven across the sands of the Solway Firth into Cumberland; these sands routes became more frequented after the roads around Carlisle were turnpiked, despite the obvious dangers (see Chapter 6). There were several different routes across the sands, but the westernmost, from Dornoch to Bowness, led to the cattlefair ground at Rosley, exactly a day's drive to the south. Here they were joined by cattle bred or fattened on the English side of the Solway.

There are several local drove roads along the west coast of Cumberland, leading first to local fairs, such as those at Boonwood or Arlecdon, and then either straight across the passes to Ambleside, or around the northern edge of the hills to Cockermouth and Rosley. In both cases the local cattle then joined the main droves of Scots cattle southwards to Penrith, and perhaps to the important fair at Brough.

By the middle of the 18th century, a large proportion of the 80,000 cattle crossing the border each year passed through Cumberland

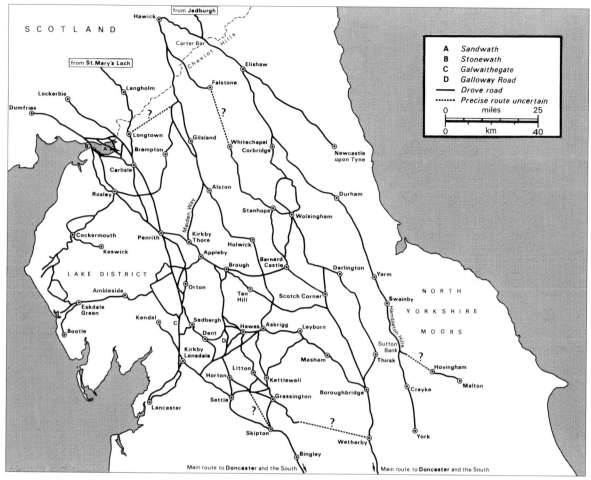

48 *Scots cattle were driven on many routes across northern England, heading south for the growing towns further south. (After Bonser, 1970.)*

(Fig. 48). Beyond Penrith and Brough the routes spread out again, leading into Westmorland, Lancashire and Yorkshire, usually keeping to the higher ground. Many of these survive as the 'green roads' of the Pennines which provide numerous walking routes (Raistrick, 1978). Some cattle were fattened in Craven, as they were now only a short distance from the rapidly growing industrial towns of northern England. The cattle destined for East Anglia and London generally headed for the Great North Road, with Boroughbridge and Wetherby being the most important meeting points; up to 30,000 cattle passed through Wetherby each year in

the 1770s, with up to 2,000 a day in the busy season.

The Hambleton drove road deserves a special mention as it is one of the best preserved lengths still to be seen in England. It is part of the route from Durham to York and passes over the western end of the Cleveland Hills, reaching a height of 1,257 feet (385m). It is a classic example of the drovers' use of a hill track rather than the turnpiked road in the vale below (Fig. 49). The road is also known locally as the Thieves' Highway, and the Coach Road, though its rough surface was never fit for wheeled traffic.

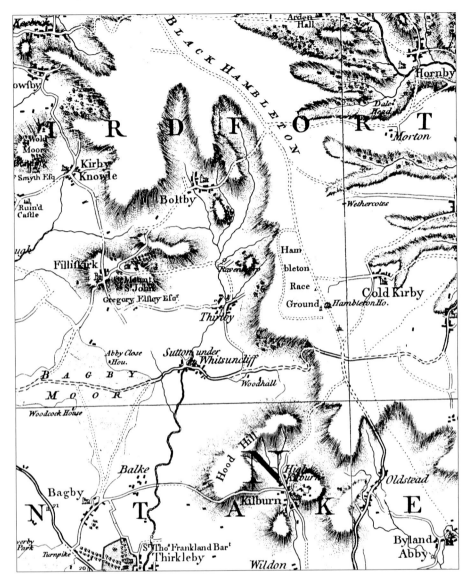

49 *The drove road over Black Hambleton is clearly shown on Jefferys' map of Yorkshire (1771). (Reproduced by courtesy of H. Margary.)*

The road leaves the lower ground at Swainby, and climbs through Scarth Nick on to the long ridge of the Hambleton Hills. The climb to the summit of Black Hambleton is heavily eroded, but the 6 miles (10 km) from there to Sneck Yate has probably changed little since the drovers' time. This section is now part of the Cleveland Way long-distance footpath. The drove road goes for 15 miles (24 km) to the top of Sutton Bank, where it divides for York and Malton. There were once four inns along the way, each providing overnight grazing and other comforts. The first, the *Chequers Inn*, still stands, though it is now a farmhouse; only the *Hambleton Hotel* is still in business, now serving travellers on the busy A170 at the top of Sutton Bank.

Further south the cattle drovers used a variety of routes, often preferring old tracks which kept to higher ground, avoided villages or which had not been turnpiked. Sections of the Old North Road were used, as was the Roman road

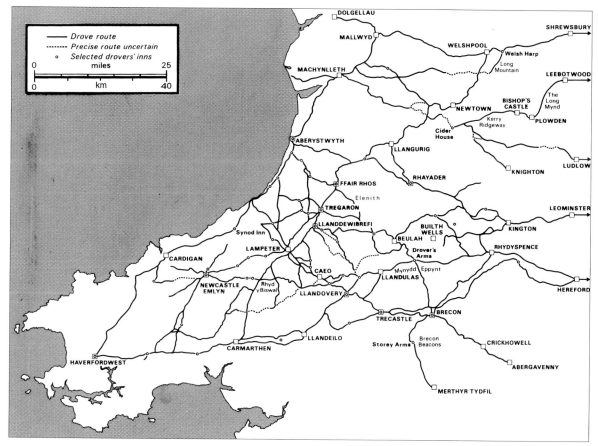

50 *The drove roads from the southern part of west Wales took a variety of routes into England. (After Colyer, 1976.)*

south of Lincoln (Ermine Street or High Dyke; see Fig. 28). Sewstern Lane from Newark joins Ermine Street just north of Stamford; it was used by the drovers, from whom it acquired its alternative name of The Drift.

Many Scots cattle were diverted from the trek southwards to be driven into East Anglia for fattening. Various routes were taken through Lincolnshire, often crossing the Trent at Gainsborough. Most cattle entered Norfolk at Wisbech, heading for St Faith's Fair, north of Norwich. The importance of this trade is attested by the villages which have the word Drove in their names (such as Whaplode Drove and Holbeach Drove). The cattle were eventually driven to London's Smithfield Market,

sometimes along ancient tracks such as the Peddars Way and Icknield Way, or along newer roads such as that through Sudbury and Chelmsford. A peculiarity in East Anglia was that geese and turkeys were also driven to London.

WELSH DROVE ROADS

The Welsh droving trade was in most respects very similar to that in Scotland, but the most important difference was that sheep were also driven. There are several helpful books (Godwin & Toulson, 1977; Colyer, 1976 and 1984). One type of evidence which is more useful here than in Scotland is the 19th-century cartographic record. There are various large-scale county maps dating from 1785 to 1830, and the

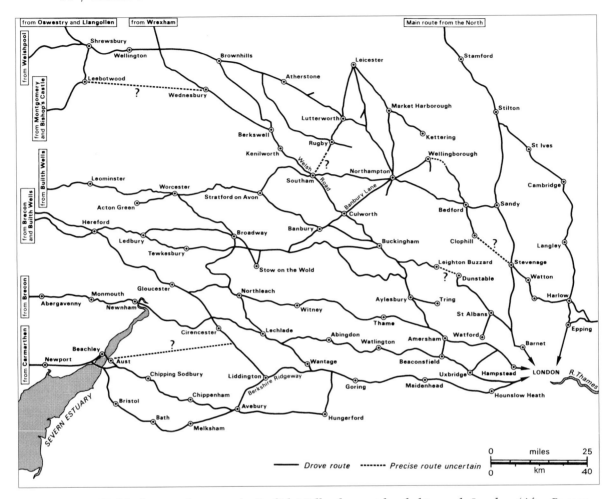

51 *Welsh drove roads across the English Midlands; most headed towards London. (After Bonser, 1970; Colyer, 1976.)*

Ordnance Survey one-inch was published between 1818 and 1841, followed by the 6-inch from 1860 to 1888. There are also the tithe maps of the period around the 1840s. All these maps depict the roads at a time when droving was still active, or very soon after. Place names are also useful: *ffordd, heol* and *sarn* mean road, *rhyd* is a ford and *sais* means English, no doubt often referring to the cattle dealers.

Cattle rearing became a vital part of the Welsh economy, and the tentacles of the network of drove roads spread out to the far west of Wales. There is a *Drovers' Arms* as far west as Newcastle Emlyn, and there are many others

in remote corners of the Welsh hills, originally well placed to serve the drovers. The roads do not head for a single market, as in Scotland, but lead into one of the several routes into England (Fig. 50). The northern drove routes start out in Anglesey, the Lleyn Peninsula, and around Harlech, and go round Snowdonia, across high wastelands and peat bogs towards Ruthin for northern England, or Shrewsbury for the Midlands and South.

From central Wales, cattle and sheep were driven from Machynlleth and Mallwyd over the hills or along the turnpikes towards Welshpool and Shrewsbury, or further south

52 *The Welsh Road passing through Warwickshire avoids many of the villages.*

over the Kerry Ridgeway, which begins at the *Cider House* where the drovers could obtain refreshment. This route crosses Offa's Dyke before descending to Bishop's Castle, and then proceeds to Plowden where the drovers usually climbed on to the even bigger ridge of The Long Mynd. Other cattle from west mid-Wales were gathered at centres such as Llanddewibrefi, Tregaron, Ffair Rhos or Cwmystwyth, before crossing the hills towards Kington and Leominster. One of the most important routes led from Tregaron to Abergwesyn (now a metalled road) and Beulah.

Further south again, animals were driven from the area around Lampeter and the Teifi valley to the village of Caeo, which hosted one of the largest cattle fairs in this part of Wales. From there, cattle might go from Tafarn, Talgarth and Llanddulas over the Epynt hills; this track is another of the more famous drove

roads (Colyer, 1984). It traverses remote hills at up to 1,500 feet (460m) in height, though the drove road is now lost amongst the more recent tracks made for army purposes. The route crosses the present B4519 at the old *Drovers' Arms* and then descends to ford the Wye north of Erwood, before climbing again to Painscastle and back down to the river at Rhydspence, where the drovers joined the turnpike to Hereford. Cattle from Pembrokeshire and Carmarthen might have proceeded via Trecastle to Brecon. From there they might have gone north to the Wye valley, or south to Monmouth, perhaps being ferried across the Severn north of Bristol for sale in the south-west of England.

A great variety of routes then led on towards the towns of central and southern England (Fig. 51). From north Wales, the cattle would travel via Wrexham, Whitchurch and Newport to join

53 *In Southam, many miles from the Welsh border, the memory of the drovers survives in the road name.*

Watling Street. From Shrewsbury the usual route went along Watling Street (now the A5) as far as High Cross, where the drovers turned off through Lutterworth for the important market at Northampton. From here, some cattle were driven to East Anglia for fattening.

Further south another route, known as the Welsh Road, left Watling Street at Brownhills and went via Sutton Coldfield, Kenilworth and Southam for Buckingham. Many parts of this country road have the typical features of a drove road, especially beyond Kenilworth. It has wide grass verges for grazing and it tends to go past rather than through villages (rather unusual in a country lane), there are also sundry field and place names referring to both Wales and London; in many places it is still called Welsh Road (Figs. 52 and 53). It has survived because it was never turnpiked, unlike the parallel A5. From Buckingham, two routes led on, one to rejoin Watling Street at Dunstable, the other to Aylesbury and Wendover.

Cattle coming out of Wales through Leominster or Hereford also used a variety of routes. Those destined for East Anglia might head across the Cotswolds for Banbury, from where the ancient Banbury Lane leads to Northampton, crossing the Welsh Road at Culworth. This lane is now the B4525 to Thorpe Mandeville, and then becomes a wide minor road or green lane passing through later enclosures (Fig. 54). Cattle from Hereford and Monmouth heading for London might take a more southerly route, perhaps via Gloucester, Burford, Thame and Amersham, or via Gloucester and Cricklade, heading for the easy going of the Berkshire Ridgeway at Liddington. In between these routes was another route, part of which, from north of Cirencester to Lechlade, was known as the Welsh Way. Like so many of these routes, it wound its way across the country, often keeping to higher ground and avoiding the turnpikes and their tollgates. Some cattle driven along these routes were destined to go straight to the London markets, but many went to be fattened in Essex and Kent.

The widespread nature of this trade can be seen from the fact that the former *Drovers' Inn* in Stockbridge (Hampshire), many miles from the Welsh border, still has a sign written in Welsh offering good hay, pasture, beer and bed. This was a stopping place for drovers on their way to Portsmouth.

Many parts of England have local drovers' routes. In Derbyshire, for example, such a road ran from Congleton across the hills above Leek to Hartington and Winster, heading for Nottingham. On the way there is still an Oxhay Farm, and the former drovers' inn near Oxbatch is now the *Mermaid Inn* (Dodd, 1980).

The routes described above are only a few of the routes which were available. It is clear that the precise routes used would depend on

54 *Banbury Lane, heading towards Northampton, is alternately a minor road and green lane as it passes through the more recent enclosed fields.*

numerous factors including the drovers' personal preference, tradition, increasing congestion, deteriorating accommodation for man or beast, the weather, the creation of new enclosures or turnpikes, or the erection of new tollgates.

Droving reached its peak in the 1830s, but ceased during the second half of the 19th century as the railways progressively reached out towards the north and west of Britain. Often the droves would disappear almost overnight as the cattle were transported by train, leaving the drove roads empty of cattle, and the droving inns and stances without trade. The first drove roads to cease to be used as such were those nearest to London, as cattle were driven only as far as the new railheads. The pattern of droving

changed as the railway network grew; a curious example is that some Welsh cattle were driven *to* Aberystwyth once the railway there was opened, reversing the previous direction of droving. The last cattle drove right across Wales took place in 1870, though shorter droves lingered on into the 20th century until cattle trucks running on metalled roads finally rendered even the short droves to the railheads unnecessary.

In Scotland another factor in the decline of drove roads was that cattle were beginning to be moved by steamship around the coast from the 1830s, but the railways had a great impact here too. The last drove over the Corrieyairack Pass was probably in 1906, but by then the whole Scottish droving trade had long been in decline, the Falkirk Tryst had already ceased, as cattle sped southwards with ease on the new iron roads.

Many drove roads have been little used since the mid-19th century, but many remain in a good physical condition, and are now being used again by walkers and horse riders. Unfortunately many still have a legal status as byways, which means that it is perfectly legal to drive vehicles along them (see Chapter 9). The increasing number of motorbikes and four-wheel drive vehicles in the hands of people with no respect for the countryside is becoming a problem in some areas. It needs only a few thoughtless drivers to churn up a green road, making it anything but a pleasure for more traditional travellers. New local by-laws or re-classifying the right of way may be needed in order to preserve these old tracks.

PACKHORSE TRACKS

Before the improvement of the roads in the 18th century, which allowed wheeled vehicles to reach all the major centres of population, most goods had to be carried by packhorse (Hey, 1980). This was true throughout England, but especially so in the more hilly areas such as the Pennines and the Lake District, as well as in much of Wales and Scotland. Thus the pack-horse train was a common sight on all roads until they were improved by the turnpikes, and made fit for wagon and coach traffic.

In the Lake District, it was impossible to get any vehicle wider than a horse westwards from Kendal until after 1750. From Kendal, gangs of horses travelled not only to numerous places in and around the Lake District, but also to destinations including Glasgow, Barnard Castle, York, Leeds, Hull, Wigan, Manchester, Liverpool, Norwich and London. Packhorses were a flexible and reliable means of transport, able to carry up to about 400 lbs (180 kg) each. But they were rather slow, travelling perhaps only 15 miles (24 km) a day in hilly country, though about 25 miles (40 km) a day was probably the norm elsewhere. This meant that

the journey from Kendal to London took up to two weeks, and Exeter to London took a week. If perishable goods such as fish had to be sent a long distance, then changes of horses might be used, allowing 60 miles (95 km) a day or more to be achieved. Defoe noted that fresh salmon were being sent from Workington to London in the 1720s:

> this is performed with horses, which, changing often, go Night and Day without intermission, and ... very much out-go the Post.

Given the poor condition and narrowness of most roads, packhorses were faster and more reliable than carts until the roads were improved. It is important to remember that the Industrial Revolution had its origins in the packhorse era, and this was certainly true for the textile industries on either side of the Pen-nines. Many of the first mills, which were sited in the hills to take advantage of water power, could receive and despatch goods only by horse for many years.

These tracks are often referred to 'pack and prime ways' or as 'causeys', and were main-tained by the parish. As with drovers' roads, inn names such as *Pack Horse*, *Bay Horse*, *String of Horses* and *Woolpack* can give useful clues to the former presence of a packhorse route in both town and country. Packhorse tracks were not usually engineered or metalled, except where conditions were difficult, such as across boggy ground or steep slopes; at best they were only roughly paved. Steep slopes were often overcome by the use of zigzags, which may have survived either because the later improved routes were unable to follow their gradients and sharp bends, or because such routes have not been replaced at all, and remain in use as footpaths. In general, few of these old narrow tracks still survive, as most have been widened for wheeled traffic.

A frequent surviving feature of the packhorse trade is the packhorse bridge. They were built because it was unsafe to drive a heavily laden

55 *Slater's Bridge in Little Langdale was probably built around 1700, and is typical of the many Lakeland packhorse bridges which formed a crucial part of the network of tracks through the fells.*

horse with a valuable load across a stream of any depth. They are easily recognisable, being narrow and having low parapets (or none at all) to accommodate the loads slung on each side of the horses; parapets were sometimes added later. There are many examples throughout the country. They are occasionally referred to locally as 'Roman' bridges, but the earliest are medieval. Those in the Lake District seem to have been built in the period 1650-1750, coinciding with a great growth in trading (Fig. 55). A few, such as Stockley Bridge in Borrowdale and the Doctor's Bridge in Eskdale, have been widened to allow other traffic to use them.

The mountain passes of the Lake District which have escaped being made into motor roads show what many of the packhorse tracks were once like. Virtually every Lakeland mountain pass has an old narrow track, usually with zigzags in the steeper portions (Hindle, 1998a). The track from Wasdale Head over Sty Head Pass to Borrowdale is a good example; the County Council was still maintaining part of it in 1930, and sections have recently been rebuilt. From Wasdale Head, the old track keeps close to the beck, unlike the modern direct but stony path which slopes up beneath Great Gable. The old track then crosses Spouthead Gill, and ascends in a fine series of zigzags, mostly still with grass underfoot, eventually rejoining the later path at the top of the pass (Fig. 56).

Another good example is the Stake Pass from Langdale to Borrowdale. The zigzags on the Langdale side have recently been brought back

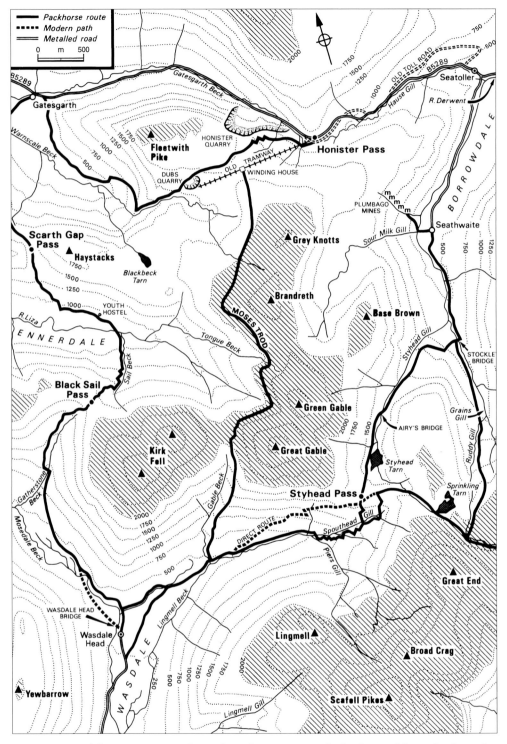

56 *Many of the mountain tracks in the Lake District are little changed from the days of the packhorses. Most of the old passes have well-made zigzag paths, notably the south side of Styhead Pass.*

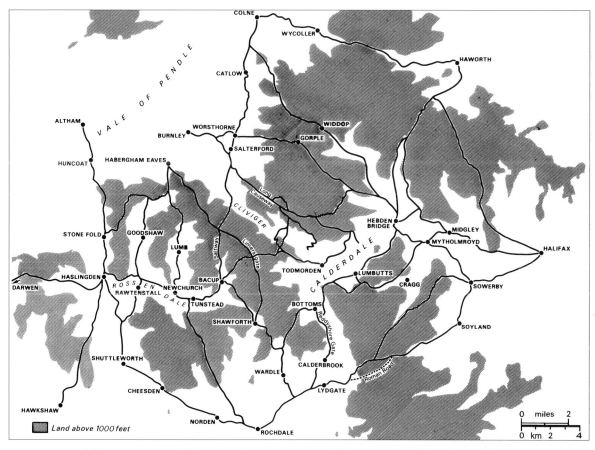

57 *Some of the numerous packhorse tracks running around the Pennine valleys, keeping between the valley bottoms and the often misty higher ground.*

into use; they provide clear evidence that this route was actually engineered, though by whom and at what date is impossible to determine. West's *Guide to the Lakes* of 1780 describes the pass as:

> an Alpine journey ... The road makes many traverses so close, that at every flexure it seems almost to return into itself, and such as are advancing in different traverses, appear to go different ways.

Further east, Grisedale Hause, from Grasmere to Ullswater, is still described on the OS map as an 'Old Packhorse Road', whilst the north side of Gatescarth Pass, ascending from Mardale, has another fine set of zigzags, which were once improved to allow coaches to pass.

An example of a packhorse track which was improved is the road from Kendal towards Ulverston; it was turnpiked in 1763. There are still sixteen steep hills between Kendal and Newby Bridge, and the worst, at Strawberry Bank, still has a sharp steep zigzag, but at least it also has a pub half way up.

There are many packhorse tracks in the Pennines, and the area around Haslingden and Todmorden is particularly rich, with numerous tracks climbing and criss-crossing the hills, mostly at a height of between 500 and 1,000 feet (150-300m) (Fig. 57). Many are paved with lines of stones about 2 feet (60cm) wide, running across fields, and even across open moorland. Essentially they form a network of

58 *The Reddyshore Scoutgate is a classic example of a Pennine packhorse track, keeping high above the floor of the valley.*

tracks related to the scattered upland industrial sites of the late 18th century. They also neatly avoided the turnpikes which were built later along the valley bottoms. As most are on higher ground, and were of little interest to the later industrial developments in the valleys, they have not been incorporated into the modern road system, and many have survived.

One of the best known is the Reddyshore Scoutgate ('steep red hill road') which clings to a shelf some 90m (300ft) above the western side of the gap through the Pennines from Littleborough to Todmorden (Fig. 58). This causey is paved with large stone flags for much of its length. Going north past a stone guide post, the track descends into the valley, but immediately climbs the eastern slope, heading for Lumbutts. This section is known as Saltersrake Gate (perhaps a 'saltway'). Beyond Lumbutts, the track continues towards Cragg Vale and still survives in an excellent state of preservation (Figs. 59 and 60).

Another example of a road named after a specific commodity is the Limersgate from Burnley to Rochdale; lime was carried along it to help improve the poor soils of the south Pennines, and to be used in the building trade. Coal was carried on the return journey north. It reaches a height of over 1,400 feet (425m). The

59 *Above the old industrial village of Lumbutts (near Todmorden) the single line of paving leads between field walls.*

northern section is now a motor road (A671), but south of Thieveley Pike the track follows the ridge across the open moorland to Rochdale and is largely overgrown, with little of the original stonework to be seen.

Another well-known track in this area is The Long Causeway which runs across the moors from Burnley to Halifax. It was used in the Middle Ages by the monks of Whalley Abbey, and was formerly marked by several wayside crosses. It is now a metalled road for most of its length, and the central section, from Mere Clough to Hebden Bridge, makes a pleasant alternative to the modern A646 in the valleys below.

Further south, Hannigan (1994) describes a Jaggers' Gate from Penistone through Derwent Dale and Edale to Hayfield. Jaggers were the packhorsemen; their name derives from *jag*, meaning a load. The route has a holloway and a fine packhorse bridge, as well as place-names such as Cut Gate, Slippery Stones, Jaggers Clough, Jacob's Ladder and Edale Cross.

In most upland areas of Britain, there are many tracks leading from the farms and villages, giving access to the moors for grazing, peat cutting, quarrying or mining; they are often referred to as accommodation roads (see Chapters 6 & 8). On Dartmoor, some of these tracks bear names such as Black Lane or

60 *The track from Lumbutts leads on to the moor towards Stoodley Pike.*

Blackwood Path, a reference to the carriage of peat. The remote routes across Dartmoor were first marked by stone crosses, and later by wayside stones or even signposts, many of which still survive.

Reconstructing the network of these tracks is vital to the understanding of the economic system of the 16th to the 18th centuries. The packhorse system reached its peak during the 18th century, but the creation of turnpikes gradually provided a much better alternative means of transport, even in remote areas. Many packhorse tracks fell into disuse, some disappearing entirely from the map, though others continued to be used, and remain as tracks or roads today.

Chapter Six

UNUSUAL ROADS

SEVERAL UNUSUAL TYPES of roads deserve a chapter to themselves. There are those such as sands routes and early industrial routes which do not fit neatly into the chronological history of most roads around which this book is structured. There are also the military roads which were built for political reasons, rather than for the simple economic need for new roads. All these roads are limited in number and are found only in particular areas.

SANDS ROUTES

In certain parts of Britain, travellers commonly left *terra firma* and travelled across bays and estuaries, usually to save the time which the much longer road journey would entail. Cattle were also driven across sands routes, thus avoiding paying turnpike tolls; the use of the fords across the Solway has already been mentioned (Chapter 5). In Northumberland the sands and the links behind them were used as the easiest way along the coast. In North Wales the usual route to Anglesey was from Penmaen or Aber across the Lavan Sands to Beaumaris, rather than going to the ferry at Bangor; both routes are clearly shown on Evans' map of 1795 (Fig. 61).

The best known of routes 'over-the-sands' were those across Morecambe Bay, leading from Lancaster to the Cartmel and Furness peninsulas (Fig. 62) (Hindle, 1998a). These routes have been in use for hundreds of years, and were certainly well used in the Middle Ages. The local monasteries were probably the

first to appoint guides, and two are still appointed today (one each for the Kent and Leven crossings).

The reason for the popularity of this route is obvious: the distance from Lancaster to Ulverston along the old winding and hilly packhorse route via Kendal (turnpiked in 1763) is 41 miles (66 km); across the sands it is a flat if damp 19 miles (31 km). West's *Guide to the Lakes* (1780) describes the crossing as safe and routine, adding that, 'On a fine day there is not a more pleasant seaside journey in the kingdom.' Indeed, regular coach services began in 1781. But not everyone found the route satisfactory; John Wesley passed this way in 1759, and he was clearly little enamoured of the route:

> I have taken my leave of the sand road ... there are four sands to cross, so far from each other, that it is scarce possible to pass them all in a day: Especially as you have all the way to do with a generation of liars, who detain all strangers as long as they can, either for their own gain or their neighbours. I can advise no stranger to go this way: He may go round by Kendal and Keswick, often in less time, always with less expense, and far less trial of his patience.

But Wesley was travelling all the way to Whitehaven, and crossed not only the estuaries of the Kent and Leven, but also those of the Duddon and Esk. Other writers who wrote about their crossings include George Fox, Robert Southey, Thomas De Quincey, William Wordsworth and Mrs. Gaskell; J.M.W. Turner also travelled across the sands, leaving several sketches and paintings.

The precise routes taken across the sands obviously changed, as did the channels of the rivers themselves (Fig. 63). From Lancaster, traffic took to the Leven sands at Hest Bank for the 8 mile (13 km) crossing to the Cartmel peninsula at Kent's Bank (Fig. 64). Here travellers would stop at the small town of Flookburgh for refreshment. There were then three alternative routes across the often more treacherous Leven sands to reach Ulverston and the Furness peninsula. The crossings of the Duddon and Esk estuaries were usually much easier.

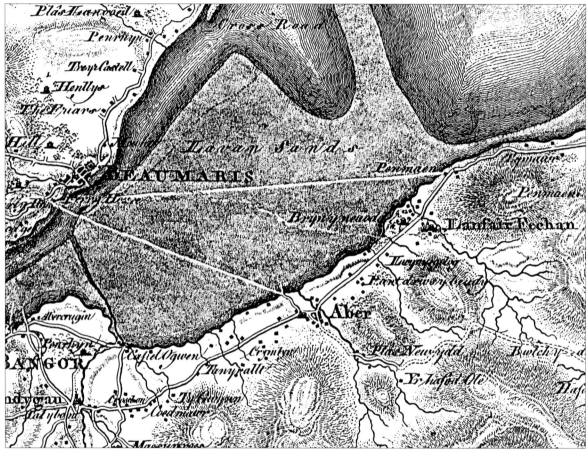

61 *Routes across the Lavan Sands to Anglesey as shown on Evans' map of 1795.*

62 *The milestone in the centre of Cartmel gives the distances across the sands as a matter of course. The modern road distances around the sands are 25 and 11 miles (40 and 18 km) respectively.*

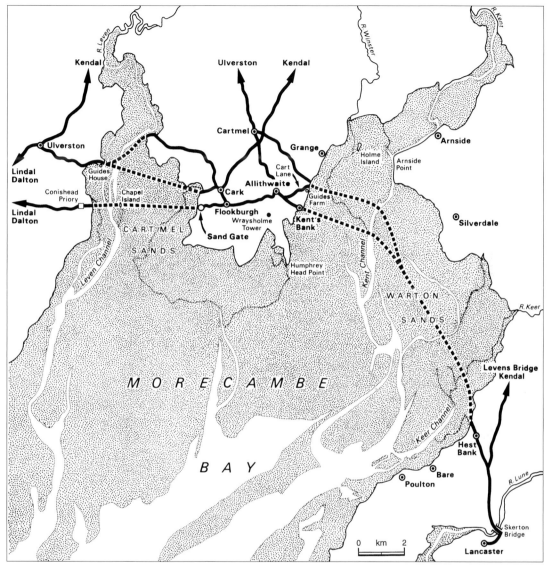

63 *Routes across the Kent and Leven estuaries of Morecambe Bay which were taken by travellers to the Cartmel and Furness peninsulas until the coastal railway was opened in 1857. The river channels are shown as on the first edition one-inch maps.*

64 *Travellers crossing the Kent sands came ashore near Grange-over-Sands, and climbed Cart(er) Lane before crossing the Cartmel peninsula (see Fig. 63).*

Even the building of a new slightly shorter turnpike via Levens Bridge in 1818 (now the A590) did little to diminish the sands traffic. The sands route still had the advantage of being toll-free, though crossing times were of course determined by the tides. It was not until the railway from Carnforth to Ulverston was completed in 1857 that the traffic across the sands finally ceased.

EARLY INDUSTRIAL ROADS

Since medieval times, certain routes have been associated with the carriage of specific commodities and the most famous are the so-called 'saltways'. Salt was needed everywhere, but was found in only a few localities; the main sources were in the wiches of Cheshire (Northwich, Middlewich, Nantwich) and Droitwich, plus coastal saltings. From each a variety of routes spread outwards. They are known from documentary evidence as early as the late Saxon period, though the trade was certainly carried on long before.

On the ground these routes can often be traced by 'salt' place-names. The 'saltway' from Northwich to Sheffield goes via Macclesfield and Chapel-en-le-Frith, passing Salter's Knowl, Salter Barn, Saltergate Lane and even a Psalter Lane (formerly without the P) on the way. It is, however, rather dubious to try to concoct a 'saltway' route based only on a few far flung place-names. Another danger in calling a track a saltway is that it gives the impression that nothing else was ever carried along it; in fact, these tracks were just ordinary roads or packhorse routes, along which salt was commonly carried. Moreover, most were only occasionally referred to as 'salt' routes when the trade was at its height.

Equally, references are sometimes seen to 'wool packroads' and the like. Such names are often derived from flimsy evidence, the roads were rarely given such names in the past, and again they give the false notion that only the one commodity was carried. On all these grounds such misleading oversimplified descriptions should be avoided. The most peculiar example known to the author is the suggestion that there were two 'snuff packroads' from Whitehaven to Penrith and Kendal; here the matter is made worse in that the commodity being transported was not snuff at all, but tobacco.

Nevertheless, there are historically identifiable routes of this kind, for example the Jobbers' Roads around and across Dartmoor have received detailed attention (Hemery, 1986). The best known ran the 12 miles (20 km) from Sheepstor to Buckfastleigh, and wool was carried along it from the farms and villages *en route* to be woven; it has been erroneously called the Abbot's Way (see Chapter 3). Place-names should always be interpreted with great care, for their meanings are not always obvious, and the names of roads also change over time. The medieval Wool Street (the Roman *Via Devana* south-east of Cambridge) in fact got its name from wolves rather than from wool. The publications of the English Place-Name Society should always be consulted.

Among the earliest industrial routes are the tracks leading to the numerous quarries which are scattered all over Britain. These roads were often nothing more than self-made local tracks, yet they had to be kept in a reasonable state of repair, as the stone was usually transported by cart or wagon. If a long journey was in prospect, it was taken by boat as much as possible; the famous quarries at Barnack, near Stamford, were well served by the river systems draining into the Wash.

More remote quarries required new roads to be built, and the quarries at Honister Pass in the Lake District provide an excellent example of the difficulties which had to be overcome (see Fig. 56). The best slates are found above the top of the pass, at some 2,000 feet (610m) above sea level where mining began in 1643. The nearest seaport was at Drigg, some 14 miles (22 km) to the south-west, but Great Gable

65 *The well-graded Honister quarry road (on the left) became a toll road for the early tourists; the later tarmacked road is much steeper (see Fig. 56).*

provided an immediate obstacle. It has long been claimed that the slate was loaded on to wooden sleds, and pulled around Gable on a track ('sledgate') which became known as Moses Trod. This route is generally level, but has a steep climb into the gap between Gable and Kirk Fell, before dropping steeply down to Wasdale Head. The slate was then supposedly sent down the lake by boat, leaving only a few miles overland to the coast.

It seems very unlikely, however, that sleds could have been operated successfully over the very rough ground of the fells; it would have been difficult to move a loaded sled on the level, and impossible up a slope. Thus the use of this route by sleds is extremely doubtful. It is much more likely that the slate was always taken down either side of Honister Pass; indeed in the 19th century the quarry company built a road

down to Seatoller in Borrowdale, and charged tolls for anyone else who wished to use it. This road has not been surfaced with tarmac, and can still be followed as an easier alternative (Fig. 65 and see Fig. 56) (Hindle, 1998a).

In the Furness peninsula, the Burlington slate quarries high on the hill above Sand Side used to send their slates to be loaded on to vessels beached in the Duddon estuary below. However, when the Ulverston Canal was opened in 1796, a specially constructed 'slate road' was built to take advantage of the new port and the bigger ships which could berth there, even though a much longer road journey was involved. There are also numerous quarrymen's paths around Dartmoor (Hemery, 1986) and in Snowdonia (Hannigan, 1994).

Most mining activity also had associated routes, whatever mineral was being mined.

Thus there are tracks leading from Yorkshire coal, Derbyshire lead and Cornish tin mines, to name but three. Some of the tinners' roads are detailed by Toulson (1984). Often named roads give a clue to long-abandoned workings. In the Yorkshire Dales, at the head of Dentdale, the OS map still shows a 'Coal Road' leading to various disused coal pits high on the fells. Curiously, the upper part of this road is the drove road named 'Galloway Gate' (see Chapter 5). A few miles to the south, near Ingleton, there is a 'Turbary Road' above Kingsdale, which once gave access to the local peat cuttings.

With the growth of industry, however, especially from the mid-18th century, improved methods of transport were required. On the larger scale, this led to the three successive manias of turnpike, canal and railway building, but locally, individual entrepreneurs built their own roads to serve their factories and mines. Although usually quite short, many of these roads have now become part of the public road system, especially where the industry or mine they once served has long since disappeared.

The canal mania led to the construction of about 4,000 miles (6400 km) of canals, virtually all with towpaths for the horses which originally provided the motive power. Although these paths were originally intended solely for the use of the canal companies, they have now become valuable recreational routes. Some canal tunnels had no towpath, and narrow horse tracks had to be built over the hills. An example is the sunken Boat Lane leading over the Pennines from the western portal of the Standedge Tunnel at Diggle (Fig. 96), while another leads over the much shorter Hincaster Tunnel on the Lancaster canal south of Kendal. Originally the boats had to be legged through the tunnels.

There have been many changes in urban and industrial road systems, especially since about 1800; there is no shortage of evidence, in both documents and maps. The most obvious cartographic source lies in the early large-scale

Ordnance Survey maps, especially where there have been drastic changes in the last 150 years. The first such maps are the 6-inch maps for Lancashire and Yorkshire, surveyed from 1841 to 1854, followed by maps at both 6-inch and 25-inch for all of England and Wales from 1854, completed in 1893, with many subsequent revisions (Hindle, 1998b). The many earlier maps, usually at smaller scales, can also be of great use.

MILITARY ROADS

The most important group of military roads was built in the Scottish highlands in the 18th century as a result of Jacobite unrest. In particular the risings of 1715 and 1745 forced the government in London to try to disarm and control the highlanders. In 1724, Major-General Wade was sent to investigate the problem, and his report proposed new companies of soldiers and new forts. He also noted the difficulty of simply getting around the Highlands because of the poor state of the roads and bridges. Wade was rapidly appointed Commander-in-Chief, North Britain, and took up his post in 1725. He began improving communications between the various forts immediately (Taylor, 1976).

The first road to be improved was that along the Great Glen between Fort William and Inverness. Most of it had been completed by 1733, though the High Bridge over the Spean was not completed until 1736. By then Wade had overseen the creation of some 250 miles (400 km) of military roads, effectively linking the strategic towns of Perth and Stirling with the Great Glen at both Inverness and Fort Augustus (Fig. 66). The roads were as straight as possible, usually 16 feet (5m) wide, surfaced with gravel, and their original fords were progressively replaced by bridges.

The road to Fort Augustus included the Corrieyairack Pass which has a series of eleven (originally eighteen) zigzags on its eastern side, and reaches a height of 2,543 feet (775m) (Figs. 67-70). It is a superbly designed road of which

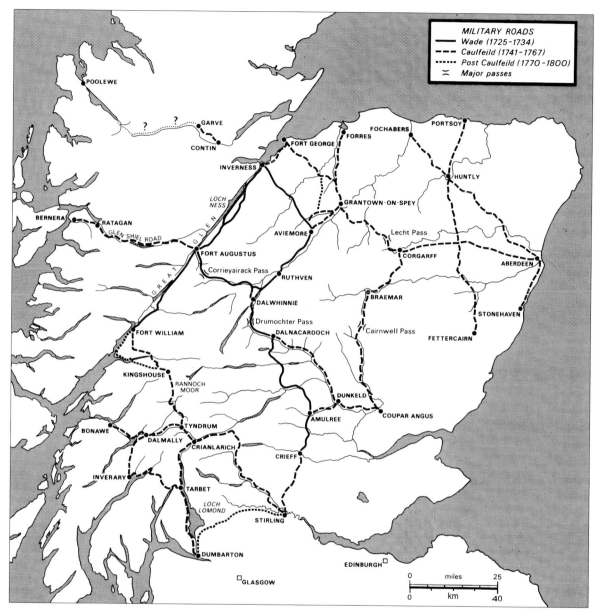

66 *The military roads built by Wade and Caulfeild to help police the Highlands. Wade's original roads linked Crieff with the Great Glen via Dalwhinnie, but Caulfeild quadrupled the length of the network. (After Taylor, 1976.)*

any Roman engineer might have been proud, and, amazingly, was built in only two summer seasons (1731-2). Like many other military roads it followed and improved an existing route, which in this case had been used mainly by drovers (see Chapter 5). It is a direct route to

Fort Augustus, but a curious one in military terms because it must have been blocked by snow for several months each year. Wade reported that it was 'now made as easy and practicable for Wheel Carriage as any Road in the country', but

67 *The military road begins its smooth ascent of the eastern side of the Corrieyairack Pass, its surface (and some of its bridges) still in remarkably good condition.*

68 *Eleven well-graded zigzags take the military road to the remote top of the Corrieyairack Pass.*

69 *A magnificent panorama of western Scotland opens up to the west of the Corrieyairack summit (2,543 feet; 775 m).*

few travellers agreed, and the rigours of the crossing became legion. Carriages were broken or blown over. Civilians, especially those on foot, died from exposure. (Storer, 1991.)

An unforeseen result of the improvement of the Corrieyairack road was that Bonnie Prince Charlie used it in 1745-6. When the new lower road via Loch Laggan was built in 1818 the pass became redundant, and it was not kept in repair after 1830. The bridges were repaired until at least 1850, as the route reverted to being a drove road. The last drove of cattle over the pass took place in 1906, and since then it has become a remote abandoned route, now sadly threatened by four-wheel drive vehicles. However, the western end has been made impassable by flooding, and it is no longer possible to drive the whole route (Fig. 70).

The Scottish military roads as a whole are often referred to as 'Wade's Roads'. In fact about three quarters of them were built under the

70 *A sign at the western end of the Corrieyairack Pass near Fort Augustus records the name of Major-General Wade. This section has suffered flood damage, and is now impassable for horses or vehicles.*

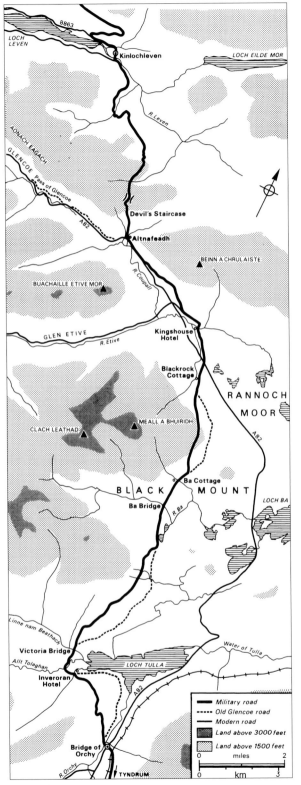

direction of William Caulfeild (often misspelt), who was appointed Inspector of Roads in 1732, and was largely responsible for building and maintaining all military roads until 1767. Little new construction was undertaken from 1734 until after the 1745 rebellion; but in the following 20 years a further 750 miles (1,200 km) of military roads were built. The net result was an integrated network of roads giving three main routes between the Lowlands and the Great Glen as well as numerous interconnecting roads. All this was achieved without the benefit of the new road construction techniques of Telford and McAdam which were to be introduced at the start of the next century.

Perhaps the most famous (or infamous) of Caulfeild's roads are those around Glencoe, which formed part of the route from Stirling to Fort William, built in 1748-53. Most of this road was built alongside the existing drove route. From Bridge of Orchy the original road climbs across the spur of Mam Carraigh, before descending to the *Inveroran Hotel* (built soon after the road), and then crosses Rannoch Moor well to the west of the present A82, a desolate area known as Black Mount (Fig. 71). Here this original 'Military Road' keeps high in order to avoid boggy ground; in fact it reaches a surprising 1,650 feet (500m) north of Ba Bridge. Some parts of this road have almost disappeared, whilst others are in reasonable condition. This section ends at Kingshouse, a 17th-century inn which was formerly a stance on the drove road and continues to be an important refuge in this remote spot (Fig. 72).

At the head of Glencoe the old road turns to the north, climbing the zigzags of the Devil's

71 *The military and later roads between Bridge of Orchy and Kinlochleven. Drovers had long passed this way before Caulfeild built his military road high up to avoid the boggy ground. Certain sections were later improved and the road was rerouted down Glencoe instead of climbing the Devil's Staircase; this second road is now known as the 'Old Glencoe Road'.*

72 *The military road bridge at the old stance of Kingshouse on Rannoch Moor. The summit of Buachaille Etive Mor is behind.*

Staircase to a height of 1,810 feet (550m) (Figs. 73 and 74). This is a spectacular ascent, made all the more intriguing as Caulfeild could have easily gone round the hill to the east, and avoided the climb entirely! On the staircase modern walkers with no sense of history, and little respect for their leg muscles, have created a track straight up the hill, largely ignoring the 18th-century engineered zigzags. To add insult to the injury already caused to the original road, a totally unnecessary new path across the zigzags has been made. From the summit the road descends to Kinlochleven, and continues over the pass of Lairig Mhor to Fort William.

Both these passes were abandoned in 1785, when the longer but much easier road through Glencoe was built, leading to the ferry across Loch Leven at Invercoe, and thence around the coast to Fort William. Many other sections of the road were much improved in later years, partly under the direction of Telford, and in particular two new lower alignments were made across Black Mount. The resulting road is rather confusingly called the 'Old Glencoe Road' (see Fig. 46). The long-distance West Highland Way footpath follows it across Rannoch Moor – ignoring the original military road, but then reverting to it across the two passes towards Fort William (Aitken, 1980). The final act in the history of the Glencoe roads was the building of a new motor road from Tyndrum to Ballachulish (A82) in the 1930s, leaving most of the earlier roads free of traffic; most are still quite well preserved.

The only completed military road leading to the west of the Great Glen went from Fort

73 *The Devil's Staircase climbs steeply from Altnafeadh at the western corner of Rannoch Moor, instead of going down Glencoe (to the right).*

Augustus to the barracks at Bernera (built in 1720), which controlled the shortest crossing to Skye (Fig. 66). This first 'Road to the Isles' was built in 1755-63, but it was very difficult to build, and was not maintained after about 1784. When the barracks were abandoned in 1790 it went out of use, as there was no economic need for such a remote road. It was not even of much use to the drovers, as their cattle preferred softer ground. It was replaced by the 'Glen Shiel Road' built by Telford early in the 19th century; this later road is often at a lower level, and parts of it can still be seen alongside the modern A87 (Fig. 102). What little remains of the military road is more elusive, it is often more easily seen on the map than on the ground. Telford's road diverts from the military

road at both ends; from Fort Augustus it goes along Loch Ness and into Glen Moriston, avoiding the former steep ascent with its six zigzags above the fort. At the western end he built a new road to Kyle of Lochalsh, as well as improving the steep Ratagan Pass to Bernera (see Fig. 103). This pass has recently been improved again, even though it is a minor road serving only a small population; in the process much of the old road has been destroyed.

By 1800, many of the 1,100 miles (1,770 km) of military roads were in a very poor state as the military need for them had largely vanished, and Parliament was reluctant to put more money into them. However, the social unrest and poor economic conditions in the Highlands prompted the government to ask

74 *The view northwards from the top of the Devil's Staircase is dominated by the Ben Nevis range.*

75 *The Military Road (here the B6318 to the west of Chesters) runs alongside Hadrian's Wall for much of its length. The Wall was partly destroyed when the road was built.*

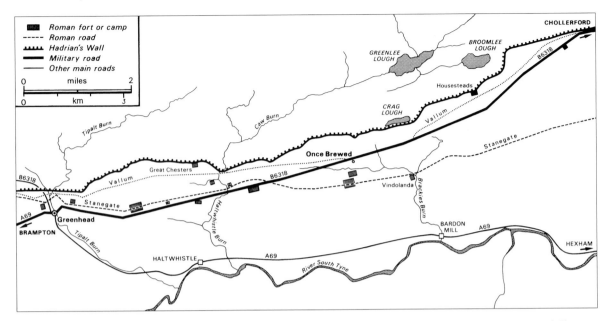

76   *The central section of the Military Road from Carlisle to Newcastle; built in the 1750s, it follows the Roman Wall, the vallum, or the Stanegate.*

Telford to build new Highland roads. As part of his work he also improved and maintained over 300 miles (420 km) of the military roads in the early years of the 19th century (see Chapter 7).

In the south of Scotland a quite separate road was improved to military standards in the 1760s, leading from the English border to Portpatrick, designed to allow English troops to reach the shortest sea-crossing to Ireland without difficulty. It was constructed by improving the existing roads to a width of 16 feet (5m), and rebuilding some bridges. It is now mostly close to or overlain by the A75, except from Annan to Collin and from Dumfries to Castle Douglas where it can be seen in minor roads further south. The major difference from the modern route is between Gatehouse and Creetown where the military road took a more direct route over the Corse of Slakes, a section which sometimes proved impassable in winter. From the start, the Galloway cattle drovers wanted to use this section of the road, but were refused permission; it was replaced by the

coastal route by 1790. The road was maintained by the military until 1807.

In addition a military road was built in England, connecting Carlisle and Newcastle, principally because the English troops stationed at Newcastle in 1745 had been unable to cut off the advance of Bonnie Prince Charlie through Carlisle. It was built between 1751 and 1758, and, although funded by the government, it operated as a turnpike. Most of its eastern half was built on or close to Hadrian's Wall, and as a result, much of the Wall was used as a cheap and convenient source of stone, and was thus destroyed. This section is now overlain by the A69 from Newcastle to Heddon, and then by the B6318 (Fig. 75). Just before Housesteads a new direct line was laid out, though a short section lies along the vallum of the Wall, and a longer length runs parallel to the Stanegate, which was the Roman frontier road built before the Wall (Fig. 76). From Greenhead the military road is now represented by the A69 again to Brampton, and finally by the B6242 to Carlisle.

Chapter Seven

TURNPIKES

THE AMOUNT of traffic on the major roads of Britain increased steadily from the early 16th century, and there was a marked upswing in the years around the start of the 18th century. By then the agricultural revolution had already paved the way for the industrial revolution, and the economy, population and towns were all growing rapidly. London was the principal focus of trade, but most other market towns were also growing. Bristol and Norwich were probably the second and third largest towns in 1750, whilst others such as Birmingham, Manchester and Liverpool were not far behind. However, this growth was being restricted by the difficulty of moving goods around the country. There was no incentive to increase production, whether of agricultural or industrial goods, if it was not possible to get the goods to the market quickly and without raising the price to an unacceptable level.

It is not surprising that the agricultural revolution had begun in East Anglia, or that the first major coal producing and exporting area was Tyneside, as both these areas had relatively easy access to London, by land and sea respectively. Since medieval times rivers had been used to transport heavy and bulky goods, as the cost of sending goods by water was only a fraction of the cost by road; some roads acted as feeders to the various ports. But the river and coastal shipping systems had their natural limitations: some areas were remote from navigable water, whilst elsewhere rivers ran in the wrong direction. Many areas remote from river or sea transport had great difficulty in getting their agricultural or industrial goods to market. In any case, certain types of traffic were unsuited to carriage by water; for example, it was much easier and cheaper to drive animals overland to market (see Chapter 5). Overall, most roads were used quite independently of water transport.

The roads had not seen any deliberate skilled engineering or construction since Roman times, but were being repaired on an *ad hoc* basis, by labour from each parish through which they passed, under the system established in 1555 (Chapter 4). It became increasingly difficult for certain parishes to maintain their roads, especially if they lay astride a particularly busy route. Some parishes were reluctant to undertake their statutory duties, some were too small and poor, whilst others were simply incompetent. There was no national planning of road repairs; any incentive for repairs, let alone improvements, had to come from interested local people. In only a handful of places did individual landowners undertake any private repairing of roads. In order to try to alleviate the growing problems, Parliament took various steps from 1621, including limiting the weight of vehicles and banning narrow wheels in an attempt to reduce damage to the roads. An act of 1691 distinguished clearly between 'drift ways' (for foot and horse traffic only) and 'cartways'; even in this act their respective widths were required to be only 3 and 8 feet.

The idea of charging tolls in order to finance road improvements (effectively privatising roads) was put forward several times during the 17th century, but was resisted. The simple notion that road users should pay for the upkeep of roads in relation to the damage which they caused was for many years too revolutionary for Parliament to contemplate. Some idea of the problems may be gained from a bill presented in 1621-2, which proposed to charge tolls to repair the Old Great North Road between Biggleswade and Baldock. It blamed the poor state of the road on

> the often and Contynuall drifts and droves of Cattell [and the] frequent passages of Waynes Carts and Carriadges [which made the road] soe fowle, full of holes, sloughes, gulles & gutters … and soe dangerous that noe Coatch Carte nor horse loaded cane almost passe that waie.

The problem here was a combination of heavy traffic, flat clayey ground, the lack of a local supply of stone or gravel for repair, and the small size of the villages whose job it was to repair this section of a major route.

Various legal remedies were tried; some parishes were fined or ordered to contribute funds, rates were levied, whilst elsewhere the number of days of statute labour was doubled (from 6 to 12 a year). One of the parishes with the worst problems was Standon, 6 miles (10 km) north of Ware, through which the Great North Road ran. The parish had been the subject of formal complaints about the road eleven times between 1621 and 1661, and it had appealed to Parliament for assistance on several occasions. Finally, the first turnpike act (allowing the collection of tolls) was granted in 1663, and duly put into effect. It essentially provided the local justices with an extra way of raising money to repair the 15 miles (24 km) from Wadesmill to Royston. The wording of the preamble to the act is typical of many later ones:

> Whereas the ancient High-way and Post-Road … by reason of the great and many Loads which are weekly drawn in Waggons … as well by reason of the great Trade of Barley and Mault that Cometh to *Ware* … is very ruinous and become almost impassable … and for that the ordinary course appointed by the laws and statutes … is not sufficient for the effectual repairing and amending of the same …

Several subsequent bills were defeated, but it is not clear why. It may have been because of local or parliamentary opposition, or because tolls were seen as a new and unwelcome tax. It was not until 1695 that further turnpike acts came into force. By this time, the problems in some parishes had become acute, and the number of new turnpike acts began to increase steadily from 4 in the 1690s, to 10 in the 1700s, 22 in the 1710s, and 46 in the 1720s.

A major innovation introduced between 1706 and 1714 was that turnpikes became autonomous of the justices, and were run by independent appointed unpaid trustees or commissioners. They were empowered to erect gates, appoint surveyors and collectors, collect tolls, demand statute labour (or its monetary equivalent), mortgage the tolls, elect new trustees and undertake road repairs (Albert, 1972). The word 'turnpike' originally referred only to the tollgate. Eventually the turnpike tolls replaced the parish labour system entirely on most lengths of the major roads. Turnpike trusts were originally intended to be temporary bodies which would be dissolved when the roads had been improved; thus their original acts usually lasted for only 21 years. But renewal became a standard occurrence and was made automatic in 1835; many renewal and amendment acts altered the mileage covered by the trusts.

The establishment of the turnpike system was essentially a local affair, and thus the network grew piecemeal. It was not planned by central government in any way, but by people who had an interest in improving individual sections of roads, thus facilitating travel and trade. In order to create a turnpike, a group of interested local landowners, farmers, manufacturers, town councils or traders would put forward a bill to Parliament. For example, the list of subscribers to the Standedge-Oldham turnpike of 1797 included 36 clothiers, 8 merchants and 6 gentlemen. The bills usually stated that the reason for the proposal was that the road could not be kept in repair, but occasionally it was suggested that real benefits would also be gained.

Opposition was not uncommon at the start of the 18th century, and objections were made by those who thought they might be disadvantaged (for example farmers, drovers, carriers or traders living elsewhere). Others objected on the grounds that some landowners had deliberately allowed a road to fall into disrepair so that it could be turnpiked and tolls charged. Elsewhere objectors thought that only a short section of a proposed turnpike needed repair, or that a new turnpike would compete with existing turnpikes or navigations. However, only five bills were defeated up to 1750, though a further 48 disappeared during the parliamentary process, for reasons which are often unclear. Some opposition was violent rather than legal, with local rioting and the occasional destruction of gates. After 1714, most bills were successful, and the early intermittent riots ended with those in Leeds in 1753. They began again with the 'Rebecca Riots' in South Wales in the early 1840s, sparked off by hard times and the erection of too many tollgates; the biblical reference is to the seed of Isaac's wife, who were to possess the 'gate' of her foes.

Lists of new turnpike acts are given in Albert (1972), and Pawson (1977), but rather annoyingly Albert's work is restricted to England, and Pawson's list ends in 1800. Another problem is that their brief descriptions often give little idea of the routes involved; their 'Kirby-in-Kendal to Sedbergh, etc' and 'Sedbergh roads' of 1762 in fact include three separate roads. Moreover, many renewal acts included powers for new lengths of road, and the occasional disturnpiking of others, but these are not listed by Albert or Pawson. The

only complete set of acts is in the House of Lords Record Office, and renewal acts are usually only available in manuscript. Any local study will require detailed research among all the acts for each road; a good example is the study of Lancashire turnpikes by Whiteley in Crosby (1998).

The precise date of a turnpike act has little more than legal importance, and is a relatively unimportant moment in a much longer process. It tells us only that an act had been passed for a length of road which presumably had heavy traffic, and was in need of improvement. It is certainly not the date when any part of the road was actually improved, as repairs would not have begun until some time later, and would continue throughout the life of the trust.

THE TURNPIKE NETWORK

By the middle of the 18th century, London was clearly the centre of the turnpike network, with thirteen main routes leading to the rest of the kingdom (Albert, 1972). These roads led to Berwick (the Great North Road), Manchester (two routes: via Derby or Coventry), Hereford (two routes: via Abingdon or Oxford), Bristol, Worcester, Birmingham, Shrewsbury, Chester, Harwich, Dover and Chichester (Fig. 77). The total length of these English through routes (excluding the duplicated sections) was 1,564 miles (2,500 km); only 113 miles (182 km) had not been turnpiked by 1751. This is a remarkable achievement, given that each route had been turnpiked by many different trusts. The average length of road under each of these trusts was only 14 miles (23 km), while the longest single length (north of Newcastle) was 51 miles (82 km). In 1751 the main roads to Exeter and Norwich still remained largely unturnpiked and there were still no turnpikes at all in Cornwall, Devon, Dorset or Wales, only 7 miles (11 km) in Westmorland and 13 miles (21 km) in Norfolk. To the north the Scottish system was just starting to develop independently, not at first connected to the English turnpikes.

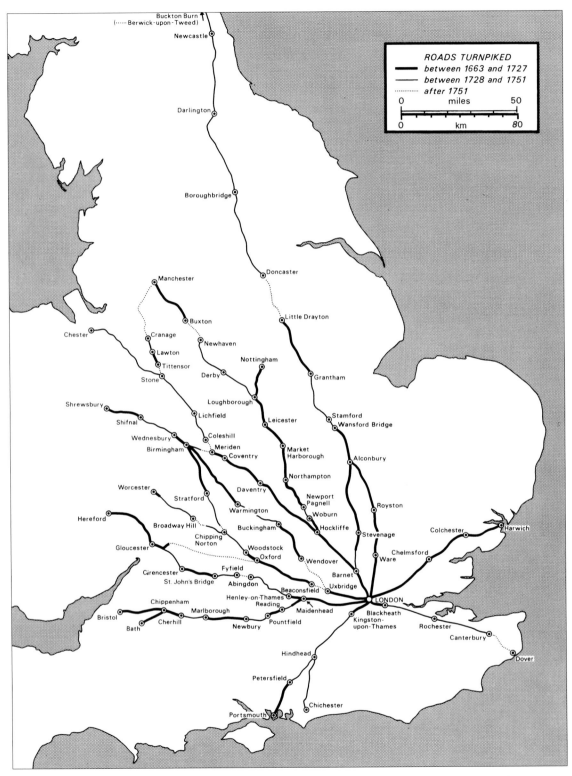

77 *Progress in turnpiking major routes into London (this map does not show other turnpikes).*

Not all turnpikes led towards London; many provincial centres were also attracting turnpike networks. Some trusts were centred on particular towns, and were responsible for several of the roads leading into them. The first such trust was for Bath in 1707, followed by acts for Ledbury, Worcester, Tewkesbury, Bristol, Warminster and Leominster before 1730. Town trusts were evidently a West Country fashion. Some turnpikes were made for purely industrial reasons; examples include the road from Liverpool to the coal mines at Prescot (1726), as well as various roads around Birmingham in the late 1720s. Even remote Whitehaven created four turnpikes to bring coal and other goods into the town in its Harbour Act of 1739; at the time there the nearest turnpike was at Preston, 80 miles (130 km) away. This disjointed development was the norm. In most areas a coherent network eventually began to emerge, though Whitehaven had to wait until 1762 before it had a turnpike connection to the rest of England (Fig. 78).

Not every road needed turnpiking immediately; how soon depended on the amount and type of traffic as well as on the condition of the road. It used to be thought that most of the early acts were for the 'clayey dirty parts' of the trunk roads near London (Cossons, 1934), but this assumes that geology, soils and topography were the main causes of poor roads. In truth, the sheer amount of traffic, especially near London, was usually the crucial factor. The road from Bawtry to Doncaster, on the other hand, was not turnpiked until 1776. It was described by Defoe as 'a pleasant road, and good ground, and never wants any repair'.

The fact that there were gaps for many years in the emerging turnpike network does not mean that there were gaps in the road system as a whole. In studying the growth of the turnpike network, it is important to realise that we are seeing the spread of a legal innovation; making a road into a turnpike was essentially a legal change, rather than a physical one.

Turnpikes only took over existing roads which needed improvement, there was little building of new roads at this period. Some acts were never implemented, and it is always wise to check before assuming that an act was translated into road improvements. In Cumberland, for example, an act for a turnpike from Egremont to the Duddon estuary, passed in 1750, was never implemented (Fig. 78). Moreover, some acts were only partially carried out, as was the case with the Carlisle – Cockermouth – Workington Act of 1753; here only the second section was implemented.

A total of 146 turnpike acts were passed up to 1750, but the real 'mania' was from 1751 to 1772, when 389 new turnpikes were enacted. Town centred trusts continued to be popular in the west country, whilst the military road from Carlisle to Newcastle was begun in 1751; it was paid for by the government, though it operated as a turnpike (see Chapter 6). The network was growing steadily, covering most of England and Wales, and achieving a higher connectivity, as is well demonstrated in the East Midlands (Fig. 79).

The mania also coincided with the early stages of the industrial revolution. At this time populations were increasing, especially in the towns, agricultural production was rising, and the parliamentary enclosure of common fields was becoming more frequent. The road improvements were both cause and effect of all these changes; all these sectors of the economy were inextricably interlinked (Pawson, 1977). But some towns stagnated or even declined, especially if they were remote from the new centres of growth and had poor road connections.

The industrial revolution is often more closely linked with the building of canals, but even when the canal network was complete, most industries still had to rely on roads to get to the often distant canal wharves. The roads were also used for postal services. In agriculture, areas which had been unable to get their

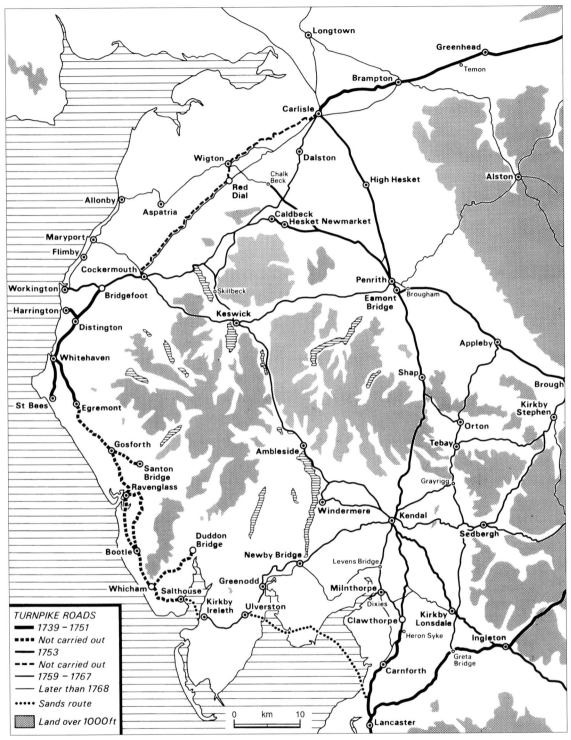

78 *Turnpikes in Cumbria. The first were those around Whitehaven in 1739, but 1753 saw the passage of six acts of Parliament for this area, totalling about 140 miles (225 km). However, two of the acts were not put into effect.*

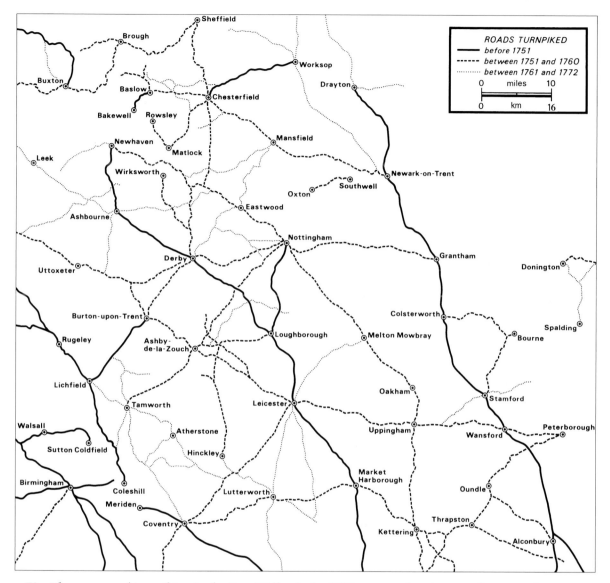

79 *The progress of turnpiking in the East Midlands; by 1772 a comprehensive turnpike network had emerged. (After Albert, 1972.)*

produce easily and cheaply to market now found that they could do so, and that demand was increasing. Many areas turned from cattle to arable, whilst others nearer the towns changed from arable to market gardening. One example of this changing agricultural traffic is that the road from Hexham to Alnmouth, turnpiked in 1752 became known as the 'Corn Road'.

The turnpike act mania ceased in 1773, when there were only four new acts, but there was a resurgence in the speculative years of the 1790s, alongside the canal act mania. Some areas had to wait until quite late for the completion of their turnpike network. Many of those in Lancashire were implemented only after 1800, at the same time as the rapid growth of the cotton industry. From 1800 to 1842, 243

80 *Steanor Bottom tollbar on the turnpike between Todmorden and Littleborough still displays the tolls.*

miles (391 km) were added to the previous 511 miles (822 km) of turnpikes in the county. Almost two-thirds of the new roads were major diversions or totally new alignments; many were named as 'New Road' to distinguish them from the older turnpike route (Whiteley in Crosby, 1998).

The emerging turnpike network is clearly (and usually accurately) shown on most of the large-scale county maps produced in the closing decades of the 18th century, in most cases after the bulk of the turnpikes had been built (Hindle, 1998b). These maps are generally at a scale of one inch to one mile (or greater), and they usually depict the turnpikes more boldly than other roads, and show tollgates and mileages. Many tollhouses and milestones still survive (Fig. 80).

It is important to consult such maps, as many of the routes first turnpiked are now only minor roads or less, having been replaced by new turnpike roads in the early 19th century. A dramatic example is the turnpike from Ingleton to Wensleydale. The original route from Ribblehead followed the Roman road high across Cam Fell to Bainbridge. It keeps at over 1,500 feet (460m) for 7½ miles (12 km), eventually reaching a height of 1,925 feet (587m), only a few hundred feet lower than the Three Peaks themselves (Figs. 81 and 82). It is still shown on the OS map as Cam High Road, but is now mostly a footpath. An entirely different

81 *The Roman road from Ribblehead to Bainbridge was used by the first turnpike of 1751 (see Fig. 82). This section crossing Dodd Fell, reaching a height of 1,925 ft (587 m) is known as Cam High Road.*

route further north was built in 1795; it rises to only 1,435 feet (438m), and then descends north of 'Snays Fell' along Widdale to Hawes.

Towards the end of the 18th century, travellers' guides were published in great profusion, catering largely for the demand from those who wished to travel for pleasure. Coach travel on the new roads was becoming much more common, and the difficulty of European travel during the Napoleonic Wars meant that travellers went to 'North Britain' rather than across the Alps to Italy. The guides were either in the form of lists of places and distances, or in the strip map form invented by Ogilby in the 1670s (see Chapter 4). Some contain much original material, though others were carelessly updated

revisions of earlier works; thus they cannot always be relied upon even as evidence for the existence of a road. The classic example is a non-existent road going from Ambleside to Whitehaven via Wasdale Head, over some of the highest ground in England; it first appeared on a small-scale county map in 1749, and was still appearing in guides over fifty years later.

The Postmaster General commissioned a new survey of the roads, and this was published as John Cary's *New Itinerary* in 1798. He had perambulated some 9,000 miles (14,500 km) of roads, and it was the first original road survey since that done by Ogilby 120 years before. It describes the routes in written form, and it was extensively copied and added to by

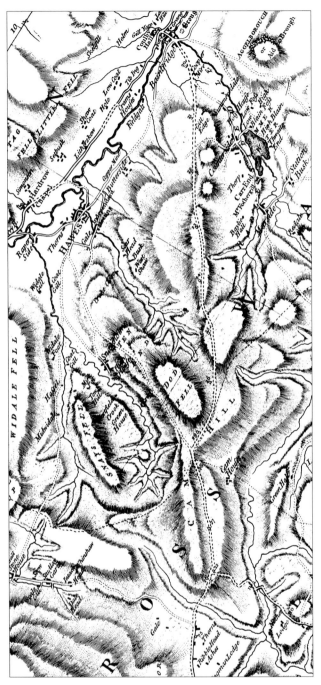

82 *Jefferys' map of 1771 shows the original turnpike from Lancaster to Richmond (1751) following the Roman road from Ribblehead high across the hills to Bainbridge (see Fig. 81). The present-day road from Ribblehead to Hawes goes via 'Widale'. (Reproduced by courtesy of H. Margary.)*

other publishers, several of whom used it to update their texts, maps or strip maps.

By 1820, there were over 1,000 trusts with over 7,000 tollgates controlling some 22,000 miles (35,500 km) of turnpikes. This can be compared with the present motorway and A-road network of about 32,000 miles (51,500 km). The final turnpikes in England were created in the 1840s. Most of the later turnpikes were very short; the 17 Lancashire acts passed from 1821-42 averaged only 5½ miles (9 km) each.

At their zenith, turnpikes accounted for almost one-fifth of the total length of public highways, principally the major, heavily-used routes. However, the parishes were still responsible for most roads, a fact that is often forgotten in road histories. Most parishes could maintain these minor roads quite adequately, as they catered largely for local traffic which was generally light both in quantity and weight, and it was clearly in each parish's interest to ensure that they were kept in good repair. These roads can be seen with ever increasing clarity and accuracy on the new detailed county maps (Fig. 83), as well as on the Ordnance Survey maps which were surveyed progressively through the 19th century.

Wheeled traffic steadily replaced packhorses on the turnpikes; Manchester's first coach service to London began in 1754, and even Holyhead had a service to London by 1776. Mail coaches were introduced in 1784. The speed of travel for both goods and people improved dramatically. In 1700 it took about six days to travel from Manchester to London; this was progressively reduced to just over three days by 1750, and to only 28 hours in 1811. Even then, the average speed of coaches rarely exceeded 10 miles an hour.

The cost of moving goods is difficult to ascertain, but it seems to have fallen slightly during the first half of the 18th century, and rather more up to 1765. Although costs rose thereafter, they rose less than prices in general; thus the real cost of moving goods continued

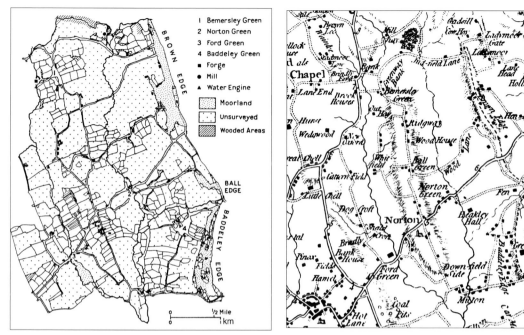

83 *A comparison of Yates' map of Staffordshire of 1775 (right) with a larger-scale map drawn by Henshall in 1771 shows that the minor road network depicted by Yates is remarkably full and accurate. (Reproduced by courtesy of A. D. M. Phillips.)*

to fall, and turnpiking continued to prove beneficial to economic growth. This was achieved partly by the increased competition between carriers of both goods and people.

At the start of this century the Webbs (1913) thought that the turnpikes had had little effect on the economy of Britain, seeing them as too indebted and localised to have been of great consequence. The view held today is exactly the opposite: travel times fell, passenger and goods traffic increased in volume, became more regular and reliable, and the turnpikes made it easier to travel throughout the year. The growth in agriculture, industry and towns was certainly not independent of these changes; indeed Pawson (1977) has suggested that 'the turnpike system was responsible for initiating many of the social, economic, and geographical changes traditionally ascribed to the railways.'

Of course, there were places where improvements were less than satisfactory; some turnpikes were described by contemporary travellers as 'abominable' or worse, especially at the end of the 18th century. Arthur Young made frequent references to the state of the roads during his tour of the north in 1771. The road from Kendal to Lancaster was 'Very bad, rough, and cut up', and that from Brampton to Carlisle was 'vilely cut up by innumerable little paltry one horse carts'. On the other hand, he described the road from Kendal to Windermere as 'Turnpike; now making. What is finished is as good, firm, level a road as any in the world. I no where remember a better.' Overall, Young described only 28 per cent of the turnpike mileage as 'indifferent', 'bad' or 'vile', whereas 70 per cent of the other (parish) roads merited such descriptions.

> The real point is that the road system then, as now, had its black spots as well as its stretches of dry, open highway, ... This patchiness was perhaps the greatest defect in the turnpike system. (Dyos and Aldcroft, 1969.)

84 *The Sychnant Pass used to carry most of the traffic for Holyhead and Ireland behind the cliffs to the west of Conwy. Anglesey can be seen in the distance.*

85 *Lord Penrhyn's road climbing towards the head of Nant Ffrancon was built in 1791-1800; this section is still metalled.*

TURNPIKE IMPROVEMENTS

The main reason for the later improvements in the speed of travel was that the techniques of road construction and repair underwent a remarkable transformation during the early years of the 19th century. Until then improvements had been very limited; virtually all turnpikes simply took over existing roads, and improved their worst sections. Some turnpikes had first to widen driftways into cartways, enabling wheeled vehicles to travel and to pass each other. There was a tendency to use whatever surfacing materials were available nearby without any specialist knowledge, and other work seldom went beyond digging and maintaining ditches.

The improvement of road building techniques began at the end of the 18th century. One of the earliest practitioners was John Metcalf, known as 'Blind Jack of Knaresborough', who was responsible for improving 180 miles (290 km) of turnpikes in the years between 1765 and his retirement at the age of 75 in 1792. One of his first jobs was the road over Standedge, between Oldham and Huddersfield in 1759 (see below). In the sections of peat bog he first removed the existing vegetation in a strip 42 feet (13m) wide and created a camber. He then ordered his workers to pull and bind heather into round bundles and to lay it on the intended road in rows, before covering it with stone and gravel. This high and exposed road needed no further repairs for the next 12 years. His general principles included firm foundations, a smooth convex surface and good drainage ditches. However, Blind Jack was an exception in the 18th century; the major improvements in road construction and maintenance had to await the arrival on the scene of Telford and McAdam in the early years of the 19th century.

Thomas Telford was a road builder, much of whose work was in the Highlands of Scotland (see below) (Pearce, 1978). His roads were based on firm, hand-set stone foundations, 7 inches (18cm) deep (in the Roman tradition), overlain with 6 inches (15cm) of smaller stones. He also paid much attention to reducing gradients, and made his roads wide and straight. His roads were too good for the requirements of his day and such standards of construction were perhaps only needed for the most heavily used roads. They were expensive to build, and his methods were beyond the financial capacity of most turnpike trusts.

Telford is most often associated with the road from London to Holyhead, especially the Welsh section through the mountains of Snowdonia. Here it had long been the custom to avoid the hills by going down the Conwy valley, and then travelling over the Sychnant Pass (Fig. 84), and along the coast to Bangor on a road perched high above the sea at Penmaenmawr. Travellers sometimes went across the sands to get around the headlands, and even went straight across the Lavan Sands to Beaumaris on Anglesey, instead of taking the ferry from Bangor (Fig. 61).

The route through the hills via Capel Curig was described as 'the most dreadful horse-path in Wales' by Pennant in 1759. However, in 1791 Lord Penrhyn decided to build a new road. It ran from his quarry at Bethesda, up the west side of the Nant Ffrancon valley, past Llyn Ogwen, finally reaching his estate at Capel Curig in 1800 (Fig. 85). Both of these early roads are shown on John Evans' map of 1796 (Fig. 86). Lord Penrhyn also built a large hotel (now Plas-y-Brenin) at the end of this road, trying to encourage tourism; his road, however, went no further east. A turnpike act for the whole length from Llandegai (outside Bangor) through to Betws-y-Coed and Pentrevoelas was passed in 1802, and this Capel Curig Trust road was opened in 1808. Most of it was on a new line; it ran up the opposite (east) side of Nant Ffrancon, and then took a new straight route from Llyn Ogwen to Capel Curig, south of the Afon Llugwy, about a quarter of a mile (0.4km) south of the present A5 (Figs. 87-89).

86 *Evans' map of 1795 shows the original 'dreadful horse-path' to Capel Curig (half of which is shown by dashed lines), as well as Lord Penrhyn's road which was then under construction (see Fig. 87).*

87 *The four successive routes through the Welsh mountains from Bethesda to Capel Curig. The A5 now follows Telford's final route, though most of the earlier tracks can still be followed as roads or footpaths.*

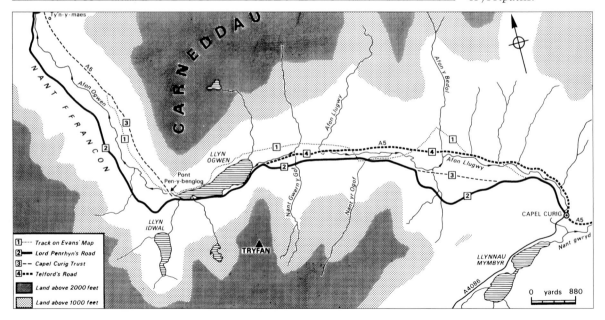

88 and **89**   *East of Llyn Ogwen, Lord Penrhyn's road was later used by the Capel Curig Trust; most of it is still visible today.*

The heavy traffic of people and post bound for Ireland, plus the increasing number of tourists, meant that the turnpike road, which had poor foundations, deteriorated rapidly. In 1810 Parliament appointed the first of eight select committees to report on the state of the whole of the London to Holyhead road, and Telford prepared a survey of the North Wales sections. Parliament finally voted £20,000 for improvements in 1815, and Telford was appointed as engineer. He soon made recommendations to improve the route, and work began in the same year, with many entirely new lengths. Most gradients were made less than 1 in 20, notably in the ascent of Nant Ffrancon where the old Capel Curig Trust road had had gradients as steep as 1 in 6. Indeed this whole section of the first turnpike had been poorly planned, badly constructed and was often no more than 12 feet (3.6m) in width. The six independent

90 *Telford's much improved Holyhead Road (A5) is lined with massive milestones.*

91 *A survey done for McAdam in 1825 of a new linking road north of Penrith, designed to avoid the former steep climb out of the town. The fields across which the new road was to run are numbered (see Fig. 92).*

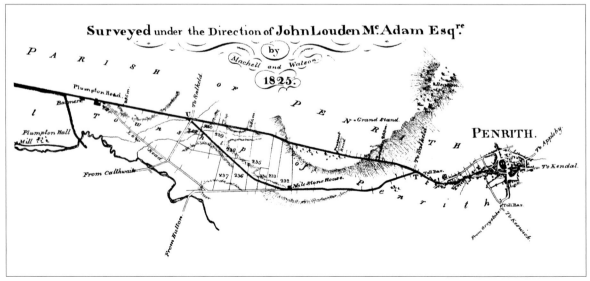

Trusts between Shrewsbury and Bangor were consolidated into one in 1819. Telford also improved much of the rest of the road back to London. Despite various recent diversions, the present-day A5 through Wales is essentially the road designed by Telford, and is a fitting monument to his genius (Fig. 90).

John McAdam, the other great road engineer of the early 19th century, was principally concerned with the repair and maintenance of existing roads. He proposed that a good road should have a smooth, elastic, slightly convex surface, over a dry sub-soil, without foundations. He said that he would never put stones bigger than 3 inches (8cm) in diameter in any part of one of his roads, and the surface layer should have stones no larger than 1 inch (2.5cm) across, laid to a total depth of 10 inches (25cm). Essentially he was concerned to get good drainage rather than concentrating on the road bed itself. This technique was not as good as that of Telford, but it was astonishingly simple and effective; it was also much quicker, simpler and cheaper to implement.

He worked first for the Bristol Trust in 1816, and was soon advising trusts elsewhere. By 1823, 147 trusts throughout the country were employing one of his family, or his policies, occasionally with completely new lengths of road being built. In Cumbria, for example, McAdam surveyed a short section of new road north of Penrith avoiding the steep hill out of the town (Figs. 91 and 92), and he rebuilt 10 miles (16 km) of the road to Keswick.

On a larger scale he also drew up plans for a new road over the summit of Shap in 1826. This road was one of the more important roads in Britain, being part of the main west coast route from England to Scotland. It was not the original route taken by the Romans, which lies to the east through the Tebay gorge, nor does it follow the other routes to the west which had been used in medieval times (over the Nan Bield or Gatescarth Passes). However, by the 18th century, Shap had become the usual route. It

92 *Aerial view of the roads shown in Fig. 91, looking from the junction ('To Salkeld') towards Penrith. The first section of the road above the roundabout is along the line of the original Roman road, whilst McAdam's new link is to the right.*

was used by Bonnie Prince Charlie in 1745; on his retreat to Scotland both he and his English pursuers had great difficulty in crossing in the wet conditions. In 1753 the route was turnpiked, and as so often happened in hilly areas, the old packhorse route was simply improved and kept in repair for seventy years before the major improvements of the 1820s (Figs. 93-94).

McAdam designed a completely new summit section, which reaches 1,365 feet (416m), and includes the long steady climb northwards out of Borrowdale from the new Huck's Bridge. The road which had caused so much trouble in the past was at last capable of taking fast and

93 *The first Shap turnpike descending into Crookdale towards Hause Foot Bridge now survives as an impressive footpath.*

94 *Old Wasdale Bridge on the original Shap turnpike, north of Packhorse Hill.*

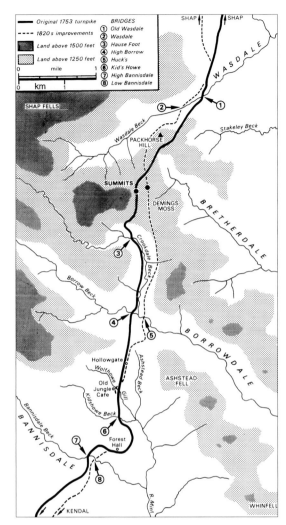

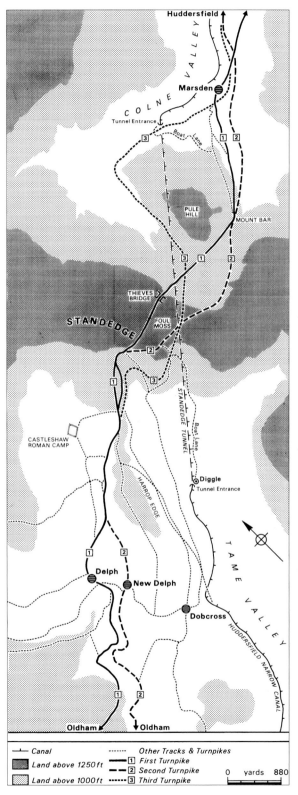

95 *The original 1753 turnpike over Shap followed the pre-existing route. An almost entirely new route was laid out by McAdam in the 1820s, and is still in use today as the A6.*

96 *The successive routes taken by turnpikes over Standedge between 1759 and 1839; each was easier but longer than its predecessor. The A62 now follows the third route.*

heavy traffic over this difficult route. For a distance of some 12 miles (20 km), the old and new routes run close together, largely independent of each other, the old route still mostly passable on foot, and in two lengths by car (Fig. 95). McAdam's road is still in use today as the A6 though the bulk of the traffic now uses the

97 *The original line of the Standedge turnpike as laid out by John Metcalf in 1759, viewed from just above Thieves Bridge. The section in the middle distance towards Mount Bar is still in use. The third turnpike runs across the middle ground.*

98 *The junction of the first and third Standedge turnpikes on Harrop Edge; the second can be seen sloping to the right up the hillside in the distance.*

parallel M6, leaving Shap as a quiet and wide country road.

Back at Standedge, John Metcalf's turnpike, which had merely improved an existing track, was rebuilt along new routes twice, first between 1790 and 1815, and again between 1820 and 1839 (Figs. 96-98) (Barnes, 1981). Each improvement was better graded than the previous line, and the final (and present) route has a long summit cutting; however, it is one-fifth longer than Metcalf's original route. The improvements made throughout this route were considerable, though curiously only a mile of the first route (the summit section) remains unmetalled today. This was probably the most important route between Lancashire and Yorkshire and as traffic increased, and required easier routes, the Trustees clearly responded accordingly, despite having direct canal competition from 1811. Even before then, canal-borne goods were transferred by packhorse between two ends of the uncompleted tunnel, from Diggle to Marsden, along a track known as Boat Lane (see Figs. 96 and 119).

If examples such as the Capel Curig, Shap and Standedge turnpikes seem a little out of the ordinary, it should be remembered that the roads through such difficult terrain were often largely rebuilt along new routes as technology improved. Moreover, as these areas have not been subject to intensive agriculture, the remains of earlier roads often survive. Some examples from less hilly areas will help to balance the picture.

The route from Derby to Manchester has a complex history, for not only have there been local road changes, but the overall route itself has changed three times (Dodd, 1980). The old road in use in the 17th century followed the Roman road, via the village of Brassington to Buxton and beyond (Fig. 99). The section from Shardlow to Brassington was turnpiked in 1738, as it was in poor condition, and was described as 'monstrous hilly', despite being in relatively

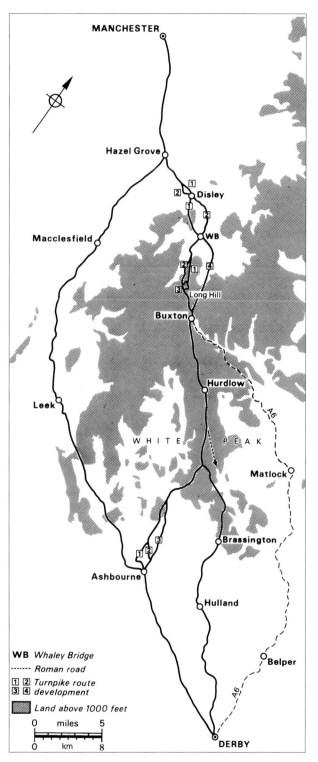

99 *Changes in the turnpike routes between Derby and Manchester.*

100 *A section of the old Derby to Buxton road north of Brassington, crossing the White Peak near Pikehall.*

low-lying country. After climbing steeply out of Brassington, the road then ran across the well-drained limestone of the White Peak; this section was adequate for the traffic of the times, and did not require a turnpike act (Fig. 100). A glance at a modern map will show that this route does not survive even as a B road today, though it is joined by the A515 at Hurdlow for the last 6 miles (10 km) into Buxton. In fact, the 1738 Act had provided that the road from Derby to Hurdlow via Ashbourne be turnpiked as well; it soon became the normal route, despite being slightly longer. Three successive routes for the 5 miles (8 km) north of Ashbourne were used in the first 40 years of the history of this short section of the turnpike; the route in use here today was built in 1777. All this meant

that the road through Brassington ceased to be a through route, and the section from Hulland Ward to Brassington was disturnpiked in 1827 on the grounds that it 'led to no City, Town, or place of importance'.

North of Buxton, the Roman road, which reaches a height of 1,500 feet (457m), continued to be used in the first Act of 1724, but towards the end of the century John Metcalf laid out a new road now known as the Old Longhill Road. Its summit was slightly lower, but was immediately followed by a 1 in 6 plunge into a side valley of the River Goyt. The present well-graded road around this valley, which is ¾ mile (1.2km) longer, was built around 1820 (Fig. 101). Beyond Whaley Bridge the first turnpike continued to follow

101 *The Old Longhill Road descending into a small deep valley north of Buxton was replaced by a much longer but better graded road in about 1820.*

existing roads, climbing twice over the hills to reach Disley and High Lane, where it is joined by the modern A6.

A much greater change to travel between Derby and Manchester had occurred in 1762 when the road from Ashbourne to Leek was turnpiked; travellers could then continue via Macclesfield and Hazel Grove on a much easier route, avoiding the Peak District altogether. When the new main roads of the country were designated in the 1920s, a different route further east through Matlock and Bakewell to Buxton was made into the A6, though the Long Hill survived as the main route north of Buxton until much more recently.

One of the most notorious areas of poor roads in southern England was the Weald, separating London from the south coast (Fuller, 1953). The principal problem was clayey soil, which made both agriculture and travel difficult. Numerous travellers complained of the 'bottomless clay' which produced awful roads, which could not be repaired by parish labour alone. Furthermore, many of these areas were lacking in good road stone, the local gravels and sandstones being too soft. Packhorses provided the best means of transport, but were not suited to carrying the heavy and bulky products of the timber and iron industries for which the Weald was well known.

By 1760 there were six turnpikes from London reaching the coast between Portsmouth and Hastings, though no turnpikes ran east–west. By 1800, the number had increased, and most still ran north–south. Stage-coaches could reach Brighton in eight hours, and other resorts including Bexhill, Eastbourne and Worthing were starting to grow as a direct result of these improved roads. But the situation was not as good as a map of these roads might indicate; all were simply existing roads taken over by the trusts, and their condition often left much to be desired. The county agricultural reports make it clear that many were still largely impassable for wheeled traffic in winter, and matters did not begin to improve until after the visit of McAdam to Lewes in 1817. The main north–south roads were soon improved, though some cross-country trusts simply could not afford to employ a surveyor. As elsewhere it has to be remembered that only a small percentage of roads were turnpiked (though these were almost always the most important). In 1840, the various Surveyors of Highways in Sussex maintained almost four times as much road as did the turnpike trusts.

Turnpikes have not received the detailed local research they deserve. There are several county-level studies of turnpike development and impact; recent examples include those for Derbyshire (Dodd, 1980), Cumbria (Williams, 1975; Hindle, 1998a), Lancashire (Whiteley in Crosby, 1999), the Yorkshire Dales (Wright, 1985), Wessex (Wright, 1988) and north-west Wales (Colyer, 1984). There are several older studies, such as those for East Devon (Sheldon, 1928), Nottinghamshire (Cossons, 1934) and the Surrey–Sussex Weald and coastlands (Fuller, 1953). Turnpikes are a topic which the county landscape histories and local histories usually cover rather inadequately, and sometimes not at all. It would be very useful to have more studies of roads at the local level, such as that by Barnes (1981), which concentrates on the turnpike roads leading over the Pennines at Standedge. A general introduction is given by Wright (1992).

SCOTTISH TURNPIKES AND PARLIAMENTARY ROADS

There had been a few early tolls on roads in Scotland as early as the 1590s, but the first roads to be turnpiked under the same type of legislation as in England were a number of routes into Edinburgh in 1713. As in England there was a long gap before the next act in 1750. The next three years saw a mini-boom, with turnpikes made from Edinburgh to Falkirk, Glasgow, Stirling and Strathaven, as well as the first stages of the turnpikes to both Inverness (via Queensferry) and England. Glasgow had its own town act in 1753, as did Ayr in 1767. The first turnpike to reach the English border was that from Edinburgh to Coldstream in 1760, followed by the road from Hawick to Scotsdyke (for Carlisle) in 1764, the two roads to Carter Bar (for Corbridge and Newcastle) in 1768 and that to Berwick in 1772. This last link was rather indirect, as the obvious route along the east coast (now the A1) was not turnpiked until 1787. To the north the turnpikes linked in with the slightly earlier military roads of Wade and Caulfeild at Dumbarton, Stirling, Crieff, Dunkeld and Coupar (see Chapter 6). Thus by 1790, the basic network was completed, linking the major towns to each other, to England and to the Highlands.

There is an excellent county-level study of turnpikes in Fife (Silver, 1987). This shows how the network developed from the first act in 1753 which turnpiked the main route north from Queensferry to Perth, plus two side roads. The next act was not until 1790, when a basic network of 17 turnpike roads was created, and the process then continued steadily until the final act in 1842, created the county's 88th turnpike. However, 18 were never implemented and simply remained as statute labour roads.

By the end of the 18th century, many roads in the Highlands were in a poor condition, including some of the military roads. From 1803 to 1828, two Government Commissions were charged with building new 'parliamentary

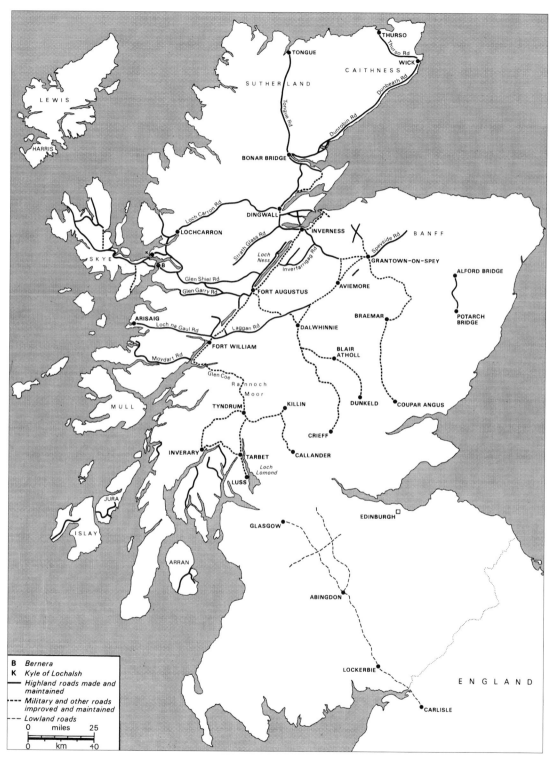

102 *The network of Scottish Parliamentary Roads made or improved by Telford in the early 19th century. (After Haldane, 1962.)*

103 *One of the bridges on the Ratagan Pass between Glen Shiel and Bernera, built by Telford in the early 19th century; now bypassed by the 1990 rebuilding.*

roads' and to repair existing roads in the Highlands (Haldane, 1962). This renewed road-building activity was undertaken to try to develop agriculture and fishing, to help stop emigration and to cure the general distress in the Highlands. Although not turnpikes, these roads fit neatly into the story at this point, first because their engineer was Telford, and second because their construction parallels the rebuilding of turnpikes further south. In legal terms, these roads were very similar to the Holyhead road, which was also financed by Parliament. However, the Highland roads were built more for political and social rather than commercial reasons; the traffic they carried would hardly have begun to pay for the vast expenditure.

Telford drew up two reports by 1803, and by the early 1820s, 892 miles (1,435 km) of new Highland roads had been made, mostly beyond the line of the Spey valley (Fig. 102). Important routes included the Loch na Gaul road from Fort William to Arisaig (the 'Road to the Isles') and the Laggan road, which allowed traffic to avoid the Corrieyairack Pass. There were two routes to Skye: one was the rebuilding of the Glen Shiel road to Bernera (Fig. 103), plus a branch to Kyle of Lochalsh; whilst the other was the Loch Carron road from Dingwall to Strome Ferry and Kyle of Lochalsh. On Skye, roads led to Armadale, Stein, Uig and Portree, whilst in the far north, there were routes from Bonar Bridge to both Tongue and Thurso. One proposal which was never begun was a new road over Rannoch Moor from Killin to Spean Bridge, intended to replace the military (Old Glencoe) road. Telford also improved and maintained 308 miles (495 km) of the old military and other roads, as well as 104 miles (167 km) in the lowlands, including sections of the Glasgow–Carlisle road.

Telford's Scottish roads were wide, usually built to a minimum of 19 feet (6m); he also insisted that his roads should be surfaced with a thick layer of gravel, which would be best suited to the cattle which formed the principal traffic on the Highland roads. The results were soon felt – trade increased, new coach services started (for example from Inverary to Oban) and London papers could reach Skye in four days. Agriculture was able to prosper in places away from the coast, and there were increased exports, notably of salt fish, grain, whisky and bacon. In order to maintain these roads, some tollhouses were erected, and thus a few of these roads became very similar to the turnpikes further south. Many Highland roads still run along the routes laid out by Telford, and many of his bridges are still in use. His work was a very important contribution to the development of the road network of the Highlands.

THE END OF THE TURNPIKE ERA

The 1820s and 1830s were an Indian summer for the turnpikes, but their demise was imminent. The beginning of the end for the turnpikes was to be caused by the building of the railways – the opening of the line over Shap in 1846 caused the revenues on the parallel turnpike to fall from around £240 in 1841 to only £93 in 1852. Tolls soon declined everywhere as the movement of most long-distance goods (everything from cattle to steel) was transferred to the iron roads. Many trusts were already in considerable debt after the cost of the improvements of the 1820s and 1830s (a total debt of over £8 million in 1838), and the loss of long-distance traffic was a major blow.

But the fact that there were many creditors to be paid delayed the dissolution of the trusts. It was also necessary to wait until the railway network was nearing completion before the turnpike system could be dismantled.

Many parishes feared that the burden of road maintenance would once again revert to them, and, as before, this was a particular problem where a road was heavily used. On the other hand, there were parishes which benefited from having a turnpike nearby, but which did not actually pass through the parish; they would get off scot-free if there was no attempt to spread the costs after dissolution. The possible difficulties are well shown in the case of the Ambleside Trust. In 1871 it was estimated that if it were dissolved, one parish would have to raise an additional rate of only ¼d. whilst another would be saddled with an additional 6¼d. in the pound (Williams, 1975).

In the six counties of South Wales, the turnpikes had already been abolished in 1844, and replaced by road boards in each county. This was a result of the Rebecca Riots in which numerous tollgates had been destroyed during the previous five years. But in the rest of Britain, the government insisted that trusts should pay off their debts in preference to spending money on repairing the roads, and thus the condition of many roads deteriorated during the 1850s and 1860s.

> About 1870 the King's highway reached its low-water mark ... Roads in general were in a worse condition than they had been for a generation ... In many places the old coaching highways became like sheep tracks; and before 1870 parts of even the Great North Road were covered with grass. (Wilkinson, 1900)

Once debts were cleared, trusts could more easily be dissolved, and this generally occurred in the 1870s and 1880s. Putting these roads under the control of local highway boards and parishes was hardly a good solution, however, and in 1878 a new act stipulated that all roads disturnpiked since 1870 should be styled

'Main Roads'. Half of the cost of maintaining these roads was to be paid for by the counties, the rest being equally split between the local 'highway districts' and central government. But the Quarter Sessions had to agree to this, and they were often reluctant, especially if there was little through traffic, or if the road was in poor repair. Eventually, most heavily used roads became main roads, including some which had never been turnpiked. In 1888, the whole burden of main road and bridge repairs was passed to the newly-created County Councils, and the upkeep of local roads eventually fell to the Urban and District Councils by the turn of the century.

The turnpike era provides a significant link between early and modern roads, and is particularly important in that, after a gap of some 1,400 years, new roads were once again being built and systematically repaired. Most trusts lasted for only just over a century, but during that period, the road system was revolutionised; a national network of well-surfaced through routes was created out of the chaotic system which had preceded it. By the end of the 19th century, the roads had passed into the care of local authorities, but one last dramatic change was still to come, namely the arrival of motor vehicles, and this made yet more changes inevitable. But before dealing with the modern era, it is necessary to look at the impact which parliamentary enclosure had on roads in the years around 1800.

Chapter Eight

ENCLOSURE ROADS

MANY WESTERN and northern parts of Britain have long had fields enclosed by walls or hedges. In 'Midland England', however, large open fields seem to have been established around the new villages early in the medieval period. But the enclosure of individual fields was not unknown here too, either within the large open fields, or as part of the process of bringing new land (which had previously been waste, moor, wood or fen) into cultivation.

By Elizabethan times many open arable fields were being enclosed by landowners who wished to use the land to pasture sheep or cattle instead. Whole villages were sometimes depopulated, and there was local and even national opposition, but still the process continued. In some areas farmers and landowners agreed to enclose fields; the process was carried out piecemeal, often only a few fields at a time. Thus by the middle of the 18th century, large areas of Britain were already enclosed; these areas are often referred to as 'old enclosures'. In Leicestershire, for example, over half the county was already enclosed before 1700 (Hollowell, 2000). New walls or hedges divided the fields, but most roads and tracks were changed very little.

From about 1760, a new type of enclosure was becoming common, achieved by Act of Parliament, though the initiative was always taken by local landowners. This parliamentary enclosure was driven by the wish to raise agricultural production in order to feed the ever-growing population, especially in the towns. The growth of industry and the Napoleonic Wars both added to the demand, and the turnpikes made it easier to get the produce to market. The process involved replacing the remaining inefficient open fields by smaller enclosed fields, though by the end of the century, common and waste land was also being extensively enclosed by this method.

Most parliamentary enclosure took place during the reign of George III (1760-1820). Two-thirds was enclosure of open field, and one-third of common and waste. The sheer extent of this process is astonishing; Turner (1980) found that, overall, 21 per cent of England was enclosed by Act of Parliament, with many counties in Midland England having far higher figures. The highest percentages are found in Cambridge, Huntingdon, Northampton and Oxford, where over half of each county was enclosed. In Bedford, Leicester, Rutland and the East Riding of Yorkshire the total was between 40-49 per cent; whilst Berkshire, Buckingham, Lincoln, Norfolk, Nottingham and Warwick each had 30-39 per cent enclosed. In Cumberland, Westmorland and the West Riding of Yorkshire slightly less was enclosed (21-29 per cent), but here the majority was of common and waste land.

Parliamentary enclosure was not so important in those areas which were already largely enclosed, or where much land was unsuited to intensive arable farming – as well as northern

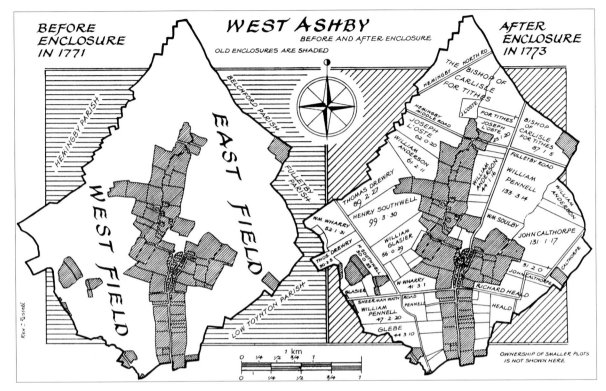

104 *The enclosure of West Ashby (Lincolnshire). Outside the old enclosures the whole landscape of roads and fields was newly created. (Reproduced by courtesy of R. Russell.)*

and western areas of England, this included large parts of Wales and Scotland. Nevertheless, some of these areas were enclosed at this time; most of this enclosure was of common and waste land, as there were few open fields in these areas. Roughly a quarter of Cardigan's and Radnor's common and waste was enclosed in the 19th century, but overall, perhaps only 4 per cent of Wales was enclosed between 1793 and 1815.

Much has been written about the history of English enclosure, for example Turner (1980), Yelling (1977) and Hollowell (2000), though that for Scotland and Wales has yet to be published. Rather less has been written about the impact of enclosure on the landscape, and in particular about the changes to local road systems; indeed, consideration of enclosure roads is totally missing from several of the regional road histories. This is all the more surprising in view of the fact that the face of so much of England was totally altered by these Acts of Parliament.

The process of enclosure began when a group of local promoters placed a bill before Parliament; it might then be opposed, but it usually became an Enclosure Act, allowing them to proceed. They would then nominate Commissioners who had the task of re-allocating the land holdings according to the *value* of the land involved. One of their first jobs was to appoint a surveyor to draw up a written survey and a plan of the area as it was, so that each person's holdings could be measured, and the new layout was then planned. The end result was a document called the Enclosure Award, a large book detailing the new holdings, with the surveyor's new plan appended; the plan of the old landscape rarely survives, especially from before 1830 (Hindle, 1998b).

Each landholder would usually have his or her holdings amalgamated into one or more

105 *Typical enclosure landscape north of Penrith; the main road is the A6, originally the Roman road to Carlisle.*

fields and the Commissioners would arrange for new hedges or walls to be built. In the process, the surveyors usually redesigned the whole landscape, starting with the roads. Some enclosure awards set aside areas for quarrying, either to provide stone for building field walls instead of planting hedges, or for road surfacing material. Enclosure was not cheap, and the new roads were usually the major single item. At Ulceby (Lincolnshire) the Commissioners' account totalled almost £11,300, of which the cost of roads, drains and other works was just short of £6,500 (Russell, 1982).

An interesting problem is to try to find out what the old landscape and the old roads were like. They can be reconstructed in various ways: there may be a map of the parish drawn before enclosure; the surveyor's map of the old landscape may survive. Failing that, it may be possible to read between the lines of the enclosure award, though this last method is better for revealing the old field boundaries rather than the roads.

A few of the old roads may still survive, especially where they pass through old enclosures; some were improved and thus retained, but many others which ran across the new fields were either deliberately 'discontinued', or have simply become disused, and may or may not survive. Thus the process of enclosure deliberately obliterated many very old tracks and field paths, while others have simply been ploughed out of existence since then. Some of the most detailed work has been done for parts of Lincolnshire, where the Russells (1982-87) have painstakingly reconstructed the pre-enclosure landscape of numerous parishes, and contrasted it with the new landscape. This allows us to see the remarkable changes which the enclosure surveyors wrought (Fig. 104).

106 *A 60 ft (18 m) wide enclosure road in West Ashby (Hemingby Middle Road, see Fig. 104); the modern narrow strip of tarmac is wide enough only for a single vehicle.*

The most obvious feature on the enclosure award maps, as well as on the ground today, is the regularity and orderliness of these new landscapes (Fig. 105). In particular, straight lines and right angles abound in the field boundaries and in the road layout (Fig. 106). Occasionally the old roads were widened and straightened, and this can sometimes result in right-angled bends, marking where the old road went round the heads of the medieval furlongs.

But in most cases completely new roads were laid out, they were typically both straight and wide. They share their straightness with Roman roads, but are easily distinguished from the latter, as they never lead to Roman sites and are rarely more than a few miles long.

Hoskins (1955) sums up very clearly how much they differ from older country lanes:

> There is none of that apparently aimless wandering in short stretches, punctuated by frequent bends, going halfway round the compass to reach the next hamlet or village ...

Typical enclosure roads are 30, 40, 50 or 60 feet (9, 12, 15 or 18m) wide. This allowed enough room for the traffic of carts and wagons to go around any obstruction, following the long-standing tradition that travellers had the right to diverge from a difficult section of road, even if they had to trample crops.

Where enclosure roads reach the parish boundary, there is sometimes a slight bend. As each parish was usually enclosed at a different

107 *The parish boundary between Fulletby (in the foreground) and Greetham is shown by the change in width between the hedges (from 60 to 40 ft; 18 to 12 m), and by the change of direction.*

date, the bend represents the work of two different surveyors who had each put in a straight road (perhaps of different widths) from their village to the boundary. North-east of Horncastle the neighbouring parishes of Greetham and Fulletby were enclosed 18 years apart; at the boundary there is a change of road alignment, and the width changes from 40 to 60 feet (12 to 18m)(Fig. 107). The redrawn sketch of the enclosure map (Russell, 1985) shows the difference between the old and new roads very clearly (Fig. 108). If for some reason the roads did not meet up exactly at the boundary, a double bend might result.

If part of the parish, or the adjacent parish, had been enclosed piecemeal before this period (that is an 'old enclosure'), its roads were not normally improved, and the difference may well be very obvious, with the new enclosure roads suddenly degenerating into the old narrow and twisting lanes. Within the parish of West Ashby (Lincolnshire), the new enclosure road to Hemingby narrows suddenly and becomes a very obviously old sunken lane as it passes through an old enclosed area for quarter of a mile. It then widens abruptly back to the standard width of 60 feet (18m) as it regains the new enclosures (Russell, 1985). Further north, on the shores of the Humber estuary, in the parish of South Killingholme, enclosed in 1777-8, the difference between the old enclosures with their narrow winding lanes,

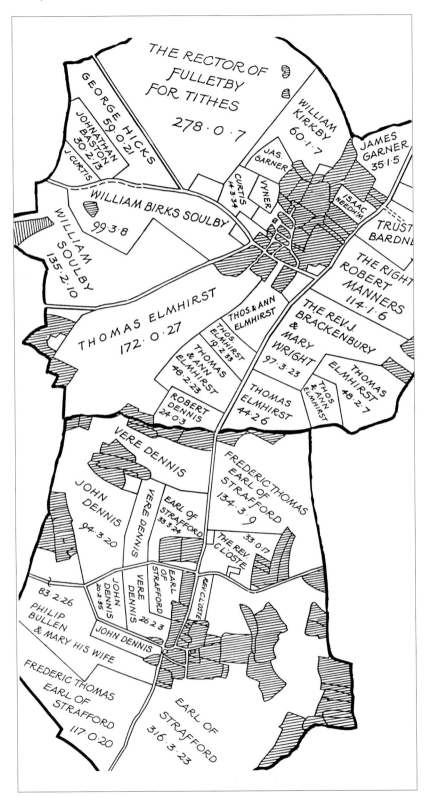

108 *The redrawn enclosure maps for Fulletby (top) and Greetham show the result of enclosure at different dates on the road connecting them (see Fig. 107). (Reproduced by courtesy of R. Russell.)*

and the new landscape of enclosure is even more marked (Fig. 109) (Russell, 1982).

Enclosure roads nearly always run through the parish, and only rarely run along the parish boundary as they were designed to give access from the village to the new fields, as well as to lead to the next village. Originally, some enclosure roads were partly surfaced with whatever stone or gravel was available, though others were not. In the East Riding of Yorkshire, the surfaced strip was usually 18-20 feet (5-6m) wide, whatever the width between the walls. At Cartmel (Lancashire) one road was to be 'covered ten feet [3 m] wide with broken stones not bigger than a goose's egg … nine inches [23cm] in thickness on the crown of the road.' Any main roads or turnpikes through an enclosure area were usually left largely unaltered, though they might have been widened or straightened.

In a few places fields have encroached on the roads since the date of enclosure. An early example of this was noted north of Cartmel (Lancashire) in 1872, when James Stockdale, the village's historian, noted that one section of the road to High Newton

> appears exceedingly narrow, as if it had never been made of the same width as the lower part of the road; but on closer examination the original walls will still be found standing on each side at the full statute width.

Here, hedges had grown up in front of the original walls. In most places the hedges or walls are still far apart, and a narrow strip of tarmac runs forlornly between them.

In the Wolds of the East Riding of Yorkshire, a series of changes affected roads in the 5 miles (8km) between Butterwick and Burton Fleming (Allison, 1976). The villages were enclosed at various dates between 1769

109 *At Killingholme, enclosed in 1777-8, the difference between roads through the old and new enclosures is very clearly seen. (Reproduced by courtesy of R. Russell.)*

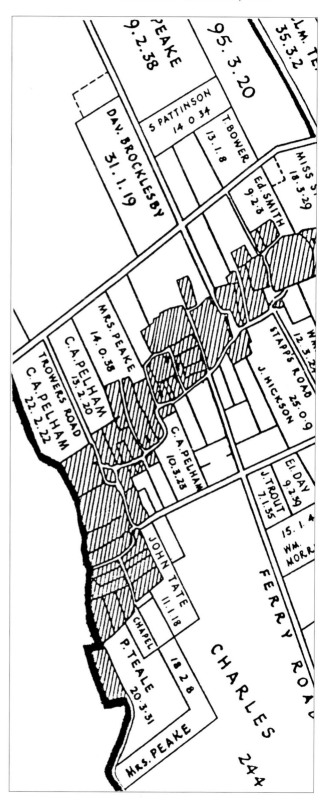

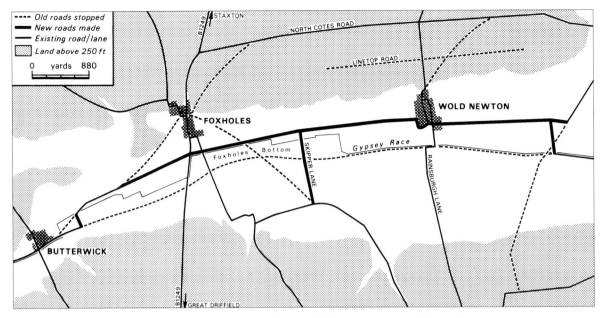

110 *Enclosure at various dates from 1769 to 1840 near Butterwick (Yorkshire) completely altered the road pattern. (After Allinson, 1976.)*

111 *An enclosed drove road near Orton (Westmorland) winds its way through the later enclosed fields.*

and 1840, and one result was to move the main east–west road away from the low-lying ground near the Gypsey Race, while two entirely new roads linked this road to the village of Foxholes (Fig. 110).

There are exceptions to all of this; in some parishes, the enclosure surveyors kept the old roads, but simply altered the fields. This happened at Cartmel, under the Act of 1796, where the roads still weave their way through much the more regular fields. The roads here were not widened either, and still remain to this day at the local 'statute' width of 20 feet (6m). More frequently, winding drove roads were confined between the new walls without being straightened (Fig. 111).

Occupation roads are in many ways similar to enclosure roads; many were created in the 19th century as higher ground, typically on the northern fells, was enclosed and apportioned. A good example can be seen on the fells to the south of Dent (Yorkshire WR) where what is now called the 'Green Lane' was created in 1859 as part of the process of dividing up the former common grazing land. It connected the Barbondale and Deepdale roads out of Dentdale, and it curves around the hills for 5½ miles (9 km), rising from 935 feet (285m) to 1,720 feet (525m). In addition, two new tracks were also created, leading straight back into the valley; all of this was designed to improve access to the newly-enclosed moorland.

The impact of parliamentary enclosure on the economy in the years around 1800 was very important, but its impact on the landscape of England was particularly dramatic. One-fifth of England was redesigned, and probably close to one-fifth of the mileage of country lanes dates from this period. Many enclosure walls and hedges may have been removed since 1970, but the enclosure surveyors' roads remain largely intact, sometimes hampering modern traffic as much as they helped transport two hundred years ago. Parliamentary enclosure provided the last major change to the road network of many parts of Britain, alongside which the 20th-century motorways represent only a small additional mileage.

As a footnote, the maps produced for the Tithe Surveys in the years after 1836 also show the road network. They usually include areas not enclosed by Act of Parliament, and thus cover about three-quarters of England and Wales (Hindle, 1998b; Kain & Prince, 2000).

Chapter Nine

THE MODERN ERA

THE START of the modern era in the history of British roads was the result of the ever-increasing amount of traffic and the changing nature of that traffic. The most important change was the demise of the turnpikes during the 1870s and 1880s, already described in Chapter 7, which removed tolls from the main roads.

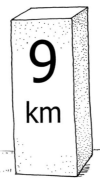

Another change, albeit a small one, was the arrival of the bicycle, which, unlike most earlier traffic on the roads, was used mainly for pleasure. It appeared in something like its present form, with pneumatic tyres, in the 1880s, and by the turn of the century there were many cyclists on the roads. Cyclists demanded better road surfaces than the gravelly strips which then existed, though there was little real improvement as a result of their complaints. On the contrary, there was much opposition to the flood of cyclists, because they alarmed horses and pedestrians, raised dust and went as fast as 12 mph (20 kpm)! One result was that lights (for all vehicles) and bells (for bicycles only) were made compulsory by 1888.

But it was the automobile that was to change the road system out of all recognition. Early attempts at mechanised transport in the form of steam traction engines led to the introduction of a speed limit of 4mph (6.5kph) in 1865, and the infamous man with a red flag had to walk in front of such vehicles in order to warn oncoming riders and horses. However, the petrol engine was introduced in 1894, and the 'man and flag' act was repealed two years later. Cars were soon able to travel much faster than any previous traffic, and as they steadily became more numerous, they began to destroy the unsealed road surfaces which had been built for the much slower coaches and wagons. To make matters worse, motorbikes and then motor omni-buses weighing up to seven tons (7,000 kg) also soon appeared. By 1912 there were over 175,000 motor vehicles in England and Wales.

At the start of the 20 century, most of the main roads were built to the standards laid down by McAdam, but were often only wide enough for two wagons to pass; minor country roads were often much worse, with numerous deep ruts and potholes. Many roads were too steep or tortuous for the new motorised traffic. Road improvements were begun, partly due to the lobbying efforts of groups such as the Roads Improvement Association, which had had its origins among the early cyclists. Cars had to be licensed from 1903, a speed limit of 20 mph (32 kph) was set in 1906, and in 1909 came the introduction of taxes on pleasure motor vehicles and on petrol.

The major single improvement was the seal-ing of road surfaces with tar, aptly named after McAdam (even though he had died in 1836). The application of 'tarmac' was well under way by 1910, and by 1930 there were few roads which had not been tarred. This process made roads waterproof and more durable; by binding the surface stones it reduced the damage done by the traffic. It also reduced the large amount of dust which was raised from roads without tarmac.

The administration of English highways was still in the hands of almost 2,000 separate local authorities, but in 1909 a Road Board was set up that was able to take the first tentative steps towards the introduction of a national highway policy. It encouraged councils to improve road surfaces by ensuring that there was a solid crust of crushed stone, which was rolled smooth and tarmacked, and also by widening, straightening or levelling roads where required. At first, this assisted only the 23,500 miles (38,000 km) of roads in England and Wales maintained by the County Councils, rather than the 95,000 miles (153,000 km) under the control of the Rural Districts. The Webbs (1913) recorded that

> the Great North Road from London to Carlisle [*sic*] is in the hands of seventy-two separate Authorities ... varying from the tiny Rural District Council ... up to the Council of ... the largest ... Boroughs.

But none of these authorities had the power to make new roads.

The Ministry of Transport was set up in 1919, and one of its first achievements was to complete the classification of roads. In 1920, central government began contributing towards the cost of road maintenance. The years between the two World Wars saw the building of the first bypasses, to avoid congestion in towns throughout the country. It was unusual for roads to go around towns rather than pass through them; only drove roads had done this before. New arterial roads included the East Lancashire Road (A580) from Liverpool to Manchester, and the A8 between Glasgow and Edinburgh. Many stretches of other important roads were also rebuilt. As early as 1932, Anderson was bemoaning the loss of many old roads: 'All over the country the roads are being reconstructed ... Now there is scarcely a patch of genuine old road left in England.' But this road-building activity ceased at the end of the 1920s because of the financial crisis. Governments started to use road taxes for other

purposes around 1930, and roads were underfunded.

The first nationally administered route network came with the Trunk Roads Act of 1936; intended to provide a national system of routes for through traffic. The bulk of the work was never begun because of the start of the war. From 1899 to 1936 the road mileage grew by only 4 per cent, and virtually no attempt was made to construct roads capable of carrying fast traffic. There was no national road policy, simply because the numerous road authorities remained largely autonomous. In addition, there was little initiative from the Ministry of Transport, which had only limited powers. The road programme failed totally to keep pace with the growth of motor traffic.

In 1938, Sir Charles Bressey pointed out that there was a bottleneck on average every mile all the way from London to Birmingham. In London he pointed out that the

> transport machinery is already overstrained ... Congestion in innermost London has already reached such a pitch that, on main routes through the city, vehicles are often reduced to a slow walk ... there is great reluctance to break with the past and embark upon a vigorous modernization of a decrepit highway system designed for horse transport.

Sixty years on, and despite numerous road improvements, little has changed, and speeds are no better.

After the war, the government made almost 3,700 miles (6,000 km) of roads into trunk roads, which were to be its direct responsibility. But the Ministry of Transport seemed to think that a few local improvements plus traffic control schemes would solve all traffic problems. It was not until the 1950s that the government really started to increase expenditure on roads, though by then there was a 25-year backlog of neglect. These road improvements, together with the new motorways, led to great government optimism. In 1960 the Minister of Transport said that 'the problem of getting

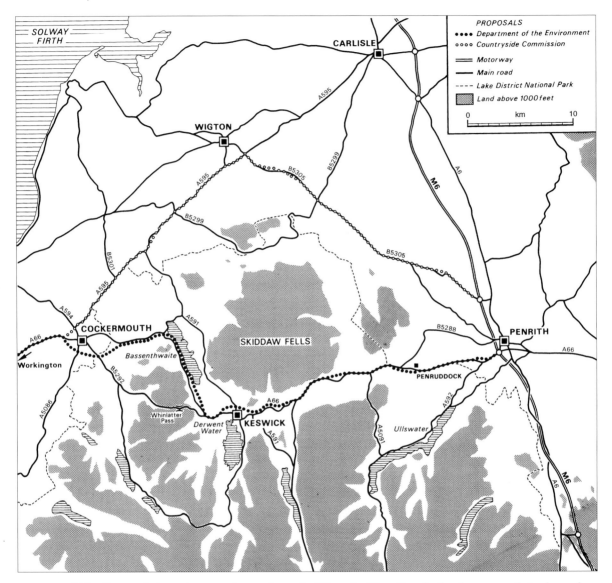

112 *Proposals for an improved route from the M6 to the West Cumberland coast made in the early 1970s. The A66 route, through the National Park, has now been built (see Fig. 113).*

from city to city will not be a problem in about five years' time'. The problems within towns were better appreciated, and were discussed in the Buchanan Report, *Traffic in Towns*, in 1963.

Since the 1960s there have been numerous schemes to improve roads, whether by widening, straightening, creating dual carriageways, improving junctions and building bypasses or ring roads. Priority has clearly been given to inter-city routes and to the main roads within urban areas, but virtually all roads have been improved to a greater or lesser extent. Yet the number of vehicles, and of cars in particular, has kept increasing, and at a faster rate than the increase in road space. It is clear that traffic expands to fill the road space available, and the consequences in terms of congestion and falling traffic speeds are obvious to all road users.

113 *The still-new A66 bypassing Keswick. It is a moot point whether the A66 or Keswick itself is the worse blot on the natural landscape. The now disused railway track, partly alongside the new road, was once no doubt as intrusive as the new road, but it has blended into the landscape. (Photo by courtesy of Peter Thornton.)*

The first opposition to the building of new roads came with the proposal to build three ring roads around London in the early 1970s. By the mid-1980s it was becoming the norm for most new road schemes to be opposed. Everyone wants to be able to drive their car from one place to another, just so long as a new road does not go through their own backyard, or cross the breeding ground of the lesser-spotted-whatsit. Moreover, many people see any newly proposed road as nothing more than a potential scar on the landscape. There have been a number of *causes célèbres.*

An early example of a major campaign to alter a road proposal occurred in the early 1970s when it was proposed to widen and improve the A66 in order to link the then new M6 at Penrith to the industrial towns of the West Cumberland coast. This route has a long history, having seen turnpike improvements in the 19th century, and further work between the wars. It had already been entirely re-routed between Penrith and Penruddock, and west of Keswick it went along the shore of Bassenthwaite Lake rather than its original route over the Whinlatter Pass. The proposals

largely kept to the then existing route, using the disused railway in places, adding bypasses around Keswick and Cockermouth.

The Countryside Commission, the Lake District Planning Board and numerous individuals objected to the proposals, and an alternative route keeping outside the National Park was suggested, following the B5305 almost to Wigton, and then the A595 to Cockermouth (Fig. 112). This route was slightly longer, but the cost would have been virtually the same. Many people thought that a fast road designed to serve the coastal towns was not appropriate for a road through a National Park, on which many people prefer to travel more slowly, enjoying the views rather than getting from one place to another as fast as possible.

The road has now been built through the Lake District and, with careful roadside planting, is already starting to blend into the landscape. This is clearly an emotive issue, as many people see roads (especially new ones) as blots on the landscape. But to anyone standing on the Lakeland fells, there are numerous eyesores such as car-parks, caravan sites, quarries, regimented coniferous forests, reservoirs with

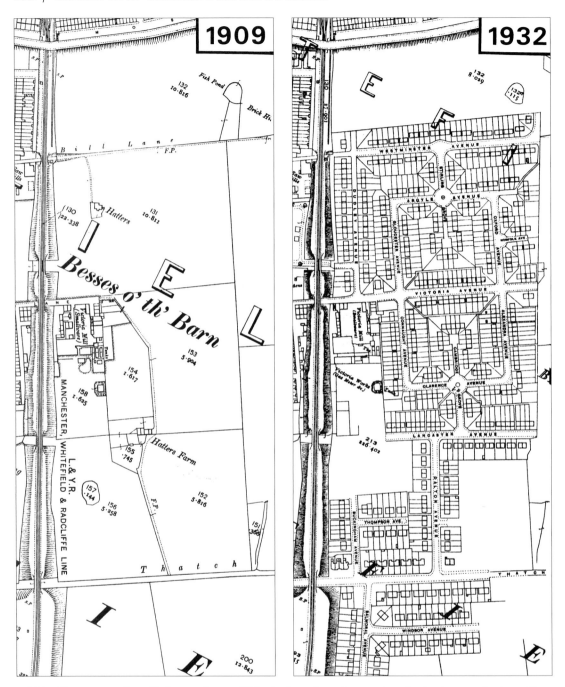

114 *Two extracts from Ordnance Survey 25-inch plans show the creation of suburban roads alongside the railway at Besses o' th' Barn, a few miles north of Manchester.*

'draw-down' shorelines and even the towns themselves, alongside which the sweeping curves of the new road are but a minor intrusion (Fig. 113).

Much of the minor network is still much as it was a century ago, but many new minor roads have been created, mostly unclassified suburban roads (Fig. 114). However, it should always be remembered that all our towns and villages have grown over what was once open countryside, and their growth will often have been controlled by the existence of former tracks and fields which have long since vanished. The sheer scale of urban growth has destroyed the physical remains of many old roads, though they too can usually be traced on old maps.

There are tolls on a few bridges and tunnels built in the twentieth century, principally the major estuary crossings, including the Humber, Milford Haven, Erskine, Forth, Tay and Severn bridges, and the Dartford, Tyne and Mersey tunnels. Some replaced ferries, whilst others shortened long routes around the estuaries. The most recent, and perhaps the most contentious, has been the new Skye bridge at Kyle of Lochalsh, where protests continue against the tolls.

The evidence for all this change is voluminous, whether in the minutes and records of government departments and local councils, or in the much more easily accessible map record. Ordnance Survey maps at all scales have been regularly revised, and survey dates are usually given; often smaller-scale maps have been reissued with only the main roads altered.

At the end of the 20th century the total mileage of Trunk and Principal roads was almost 30,000 miles (48,200 km). But the total length of minor roads was much greater; there are over 70,000 miles (113,000 km) of B and C roads, plus almost 130,000 miles (207,000km) which are unclassified. The total length of all roads was just over 230,000 miles (372,000 km).

MOTORWAYS

The single greatest change to the road system in the 20th century has been the creation of motorways. The notion of such totally new roads was being aired in the early 1920s. Hilaire Belloc (1923) said that the railways had defeated a scheme in which new arterial roads would have linked the main centres of population. New motorways were already being built in Italy, Germany and the USA in the period between the two World Wars, yet nothing along these lines was done in Britain, despite plentiful labour supplies due to the high levels of unemployment. The Institution of Highway Engineers and then the County Surveyors' Society put forward detailed proposals in 1936 and 1938, and the post-war government finally announced its motorway proposals in 1946 (Fig. 115). It was proposed to start work in 1951, and an enabling act was passed in 1949, but it was not until 1956 that the first motorway construction was begun.

The process of building a motorway was long and complicated. First the need for a particular length of motorway had to be justified (usually on grounds of existing congested roads), and money had to be made available. Then a route had to be chosen and a public enquiry held, the road was then designed, the land was purchased (often by compulsion), and compensation terms agreed, before construction could begin. In addition, many existing features, including other roads and footpaths, had to be altered.

The first short stretch of the M6, opened in 1958, was little more than a restricted access bypass for the A6 around Preston (see Yeadon's chapter in Crosby, 1998). But in the following year the first major length of motorway was opened, namely the M1 from Watford to Crick in Northamptonshire, where it joined the A5 (i.e. the Roman Watling Street!). These new roads were intended to allow rapid and safe long-distance movement. They increased capacity, had limited access points, excluded pedestrians, cyclists and various slow vehicles, and did not interfere much with existing roads during their construction. Furthermore it was hoped that they would leave the 'old roads' for cyclists and local traffic. All this was thought to be better than widening or dualling the existing main roads.

In the space of forty years, the motorway network has grown dramatically. The completion of London's 'Motorway Box', the M25, was one of the most expensive and controversial

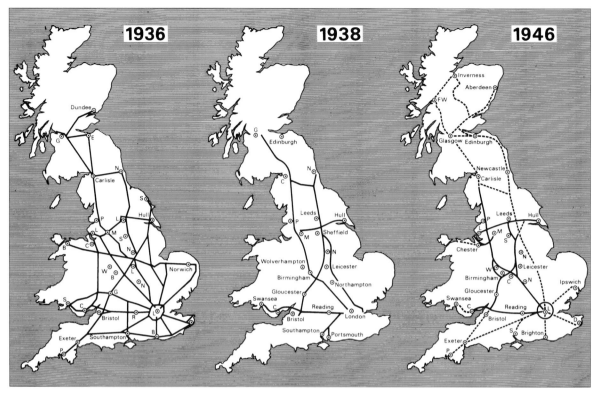

115 *Three proposals for the British motorway system, 1936-46. It is interesting to compare these plans with what has now been built.*

schemes; known unkindly as London's 'orbital car-park', it was soon heavily used, often congested and needed improving. Manchester's orbital motorway, the M60, was not completed until 2000, over 35 years after its first sections were opened.

In 1990 the government announced its intention to build the missing section of the M3 near Winchester across Twyford Down, rather than tunnelling beneath it. The predictable local (and national) outcry followed immediately, even though the scheme involved digging up the existing bypass and returning it to nature. This last event is a very unusual step indeed; very rarely in the long history of roads has a perfectly good road been taken out of use deliberately.

Only a few months later, a leaked draft of a possible route for the Greater Manchester West-ern and Northern Relief Roads immediately raised much opposition. It was proposed to build these new motorways from the M6 at Knutsford across north Manchester to the M66, running parallel to the existing M62 (which was to be widened to four lanes each way; now renamed as part of the M60). The new road would have run through many housing and recreational areas; it now appears extremely unlikely that either road will be built.

A dramatic change of policy occurred during the 1990s, when many schemes for motorway building were scrapped. In the three years 1991-4, 327 miles (526 km) of motorway were begun, but in 1997-2000 the figure was only 19 miles (30 km). The total length of motorways at the end of the 20th century was just over 2,100 miles (3,400 km). British motorways are toll-free, and it is interesting to speculate whether we may have now had a greater mileage of motorways if tolls had provided extra money, as has happened in France and Germany.

Despite the 1946 plan, and various subsequent proposals, the network has grown without a detailed master plan. There are some stretches which are grossly overloaded, while others see much less traffic. There are clearly also certain routes which have not yet been provided with motorway links; the most obvious is from Manchester to Sheffield, the two largest conurbations not yet connected by a motorway. There are two existing routes (Snake Pass, A57, and Woodhead Pass, A628) most of which are not even dual carriageway. But whether it would now be environmentally possible to build such a new motorway link across the Pennines, probably involving tunnelling, is very doubtful. Other missing links are Birmingham to Southampton (now a mixture of motorway and dual carriageway), and the route from the Midlands to East Anglia, first proposed in 1936 (now a dual carriageway). We have reached the stage where it is difficult to imagine the existing motorway network being built at all under present conditions. Projects such as the magnificent route of the M6 through the Lune Gorge would surely be opposed were they to be proposed today.

Nevertheless, the recent development of towns, housing, shopping and industry has been radically affected by the location of the motorways; proximity to a motorway access point or junction can prove a valuable asset to some, and a nuisance to others. In particular, the development of out-of-town shopping centres owes much to increased car ownership and the motorways; Meadowhall in Sheffield and the Trafford Centre in Manchester are just two examples of such centres adjacent to motorway junctions.

An alternative strategy has been to upgrade certain existing roads, rather than build totally new ones; the classic example is the A1/A1(M) from London to Tyneside, which was made into a mixture of motorway and dual carriageway beginning in the early 1960s. By 1990 over a quarter of its length was motorway, and more of the route was upgraded during the 1990s, though not as much as had been planned; much is still an A-road. A similar idea to improve the A4 instead of building the M4 was rejected many years ago and the A4 still survives largely intact.

Motorways are important landscape features in their own right. No doubt the Tinsley viaduct carrying the M1 past Sheffield, or the Barton high-level bridge taking the M60 over the Manchester Ship Canal will stand as monuments to the road architecture of the late 20th century. The two curving levels of the M6 as it passes through the Lune Gorge (Fig. 116), the dramatic crossing of the Pennines by the M62 (Fig. 117), and the way in which the M5 climbs the ridge south of Bristol are other good examples. James Drake (1969), a noted County Surveyor responsible for many of the early motorways in Lancashire, demonstrated his enthusiasm clearly:

> The building of a motorway is sculpture on an exciting grand scale, carving, moulding and adapting ... earth, rock and minerals into a finished product, which must be both functional and pleasing to the eye, as well as economical and durable.

FOOTPATHS

Many tracks and lesser routes have gone out of use, been ploughed out or built over. Nevertheless, there are some 140,000 miles (225,000km) of public footpaths, bridleways and byways in England and Wales. The basic legal distinction between these three types of right of way is that footpaths are for walkers only, bridleways may also be used by cyclists and horse riders, whilst byways (often green roads or other old roads) are open to all traffic, including mechanically propelled vehicles. The Countryside and Rights of Way Act 2000 automatically reclassified the

116 *The M6 curving its way through the Lune Gorge adds an architectural layer to the landscape.*

117 *The summit cutting of the M62 crossing the Pennines, taken from the Pennine Way footbridge.*

obscure RUPPS (Roads Used as Public Paths) as restricted byways (not available to mechanically propelled vehicles). The situation in Scotland is somewhat less precise, partly because there is much more open country than exists south of the border; the Scottish Rights of Way Society was formed to defend footpath access in Scotland.

Definitive footpath maps for all counties of England and Wales, and for some in Scotland, should be kept up to date by the local highway authority. Ordnance Survey maps (1:25,000 and 1:50,000) also show rights of way, though they are always at least a little out of date, and thus not quite as reliable as the definitive maps. The 1:25,000 scale maps are, in fact, called 'Pathfinder' maps; they show rights of way in green. There is no shortage of published footpath guides, as a visit to any good bookshop will show. The maintenance of all these tracks is normally the responsibility of the County Councils, though they may delegate the job to District or Parish Councils, or to the National Park authorities. In practice this can sometimes lead to confusion, with each leaving the job to the others.

The idea of creating long-distance footpaths or National Trails, was made possible by an Act of 1949. These paths are in many ways the footpath equivalent of the motorways, except that they are largely based on existing rights of way. The first to be designated was the 270-mile (435 km) Pennine Way; originally suggested in 1935, it was finally 'opened' in 1965 (Stephenson, 1969). It has since been followed by many more, with several following old routes, including the Ridgeway Path, the Norfolk Coast Path (which includes the Peddar's Way), the North Downs Way (the Pilgrims' Way) and the West Highland Way (partly drove road, military road and turnpike). Others are purely modern inventions. Offa's Dyke Path, for example, follows the eighth-century defensive line, while the Pembrokeshire Coast Path forms the backbone of a National Park. One of the longest is the South-West Peninsula Coast Path, at 515 miles (830 km).

There are now many other long-distance routes; 545 are listed in the latest edition of the *Long Distance Walker's Handbook*. Most are described officially as Recreational Paths, and their origins are often due to the efforts of ramblers, local authorities or voluntary groups and their creation and management may be supported financially by the Countryside Commission. These paths vary enormously in length. Some are quite long, such as the 190 mile (306 km) Coast to Coast Path from St Bees to Robin Hood's Bay, though many are much shorter. A shorter route is the Irwell Valley Way, which runs for 30 miles (48 km), close to the river from Manchester to its source above Bacup. Shorter routes are referred to as Local Walks or Parish Paths; some are specifically designed as circular day walks, with the car driver very much in mind. Of course, even on the long routes, most people simply walk short sections – the number of people going for day walks on parts of the Pennine Way far outnumbers the few who walk its entire length.

A recent phenomenon is the 'Challenge Walk', in which walkers are challenged to walk a particular route on a specific day; badges or certificates may be available for completing these walks. They tend to encourage speed and over-use rather than leisure, and may cause excessive footpath erosion. One of the best known is the 24-mile (39 km) Three Peaks Walk which takes in the summits of Ingleborough, Whernside and Pen-y-Ghent.

Finally, there are canal towpaths (most of which are usable, even if the canal is not), and the entirely new footpaths created where abandoned railway lines have been turned into walks or nature trails (Fig. 118).

A problem encountered by many of these routes is that it is difficult and often expensive to create new rights of way and those planning new routes try to use existing rights of way wherever possible, as many landowners are

118 *The towpath of the Manchester, Bolton and Bury Canal at Nob End has become part of the local footpath network.*

very reluctant to grant new access routes across their land. There is an obvious potential conflict between recreation and farming, as seen during the Foot and Mouth Disease outbreak in 2001. Footpaths can also hinder conservation and preservation of the countryside; but more often, landowners simply wish to keep people off their land. Thus recreational paths sometimes take rather odd routes, avoiding private land.

Rights of way may also be extinguished if they are no longer needed, though local voluntary groups usually object to any such proposal by a landowner. A special case is where land is used by the Ministry of Defence; here routes have been lost on a temporary or even permanent basis, often due to the use of live ammunition. Notable areas where this has happened include large areas of Salisbury Plain, Dartmoor and south Pembrokeshire, as well as numerous small sites throughout the country.

Large tracts of Britain have no rights of way at all, and access to such areas is at the whim of the owners; this is especially true in Scotland. Many landowners simply accept customary usage, but a few actively seek to restrict access. A good example is to be found on Casterton and Leck Fells, near Kirkby Lonsdale, beneath

which lies the largest cave system in Britain. There are no rights of way across the fells, other than the two roads to the highest farms, and both landowners have placed severe restrictions on those wishing to visit the numerous caves.

The Countryside and Rights of Way Act 2000 finally granted the freedom to roam over mountain, moor, heath, down and common land in England and Wales. Its provisions will take several years to come into effect, principally because new maps have to be drawn up to show the access land.

Historians may also be interested in trying to establish whether a particular route has been and remains a right of way. This is an extremely complex topic, but fortunately Riddall and Trevelyan (1992) is the definitive text. They look in turn at the nature of rights of way and how they come into being, definitive maps and other records, changes to the network, obstructions and other nuisances, maintenance and improvement, and also give advice on 'things you can do'. The only drawback is that the book predates the 2000 Act; hopefully a revised version will appear soon.

The ordinary walker is often faced with problems such as blocked or overgrown paths or barbed wire, as well as farmers who do not reinstate paths within two weeks of ploughing or who (legally or illegally) keep certain breeds of bulls in fields crossed by rights of way. A Countryside Commission survey of 1988 found that over half the rights of way in England and Wales were impossible to follow without the use of a map. Two-thirds were not signposted where they left a road (as required by law), and 1 in 6 were difficult or impossible to follow, even with a map. And all this assumes that the average walker can in fact read a map in the very precise manner required to locate and follow a footpath which is not clear on the ground.

Despite these problems, walking is now without doubt the most popular form of countryside recreation, and the increasing number of footpath signs reflects the greater leisure use of these old rights of way (Fig. 119). But certain footpaths, so long neglected as a recreational resource, have now become seriously over-used. Some of the tracks up Snowdon and many of those in the Lake District have become scars on the landscape, and have had to be reinforced with stone chippings, rebuilt or even rerouted. A very different solution has been adopted in the case of the Lyke Wake Walk across the North York Moors, which once reputedly saw over 40,000 walkers in a single year. It has now been removed from many lists of walks and from maps in an attempt to reverse the damage.

In 1995 the creation of the National Cycle Network was begun, with the aim of establishing a 10,000 mile (16,000 km) network of cycle tracks by 2005; the first half was officially opened in June 2000. It is being undertaken by the charity Sustrans (sustainable transport), and is funded by lottery money. More generally, Sustrans works on projects to encourage people to walk and cycle more, to help reduce motor traffic and its adverse effects.

Another problem is the increasing use of mountain bikes; they may be ridden on bridleways and byways, but their use on footpaths is illegal, as it is on the hills themselves (unless the owner has given express permission). It is rather curious that these bikes are named after part of the landscape where they often should not be used! But rather more serious is the use of motorbikes and four-wheel drive vehicles on unsurfaced tracks (Fig. 120). The use of these vehicles may or may not be illegal, depending on the legal status of the track involved, but a great deal of damage can be done to ancient tracks in a very short time, making them difficult or impassable for other more traditional users.

THE FUTURE

It is always dangerous to try to predict what may happen in the future. Writing in 1971, Hindley thought that by the end of the century, moving pavements and transporters

119 *A variety of footpath and right of way signs.*

would be in general use, freight and people would travel by pipelines, electric cars would be universal, and that town cars would be silent cubes. He believed that computers would control the movement of all town traffic, and that vehicles would be hovercraft or use magnetic suspension rather than wheels. Instead, the private car is clearly here to stay; it offers so many advantages that it is unlikely to be surrendered voluntarily in the foreseeable future. It has already changed so many attitudes, and has affected the growth and planning of numerous aspects of life. The places in which we live, work, shop and enjoy ourselves have all been drastically changed.

British roads are becoming ever more congested, and traffic speeds are falling, especially in towns, largely because of the ever-increasing levels of car ownership and use which have continued to grow faster than the available road capacity. Solutions to this problem involve both improving the infrastructure of roads and trying to reduce the amount of traffic. But supply and demand are not independent of each other – widening or building a new road obviously creates more capacity, but it also generates new traffic.

Improving roads has for the last hundred years been controlled by the level of government spending. The current strategy is to widen a few existing roads. At worst this will provide only a short-term set of better routes between traffic jams. There are limits to the number of new roads and improvements that can be made; Britain already has more tarmac per square mile than any other country in the world apart from Belgium. Matters are worst in towns where there is a conflict between retaining the urban fabric and making room for the private car.

There is one scheme for a new road, the Birmingham North Relief Road, which is due to be built in the early 2000s; privately financed, this will be a toll road, marking a return to the turnpike system. There are no plans for general motorway tolls in the near future.

Reducing the demand might be achieved by such measures as charging people more for simply owning a car, or discouraging the issue, use and subsidy of company cars. The government always has the option of charging road users for travelling by increasing fuel taxes, but this is politically a very sensitive issue. The Transport Act (2000) gives local authorities the possibility of introducing road pricing (congestion tolls) or workplace parking levies; most of the money raised would be spent on improving public transport. Alternatively, the number of commuters could be reduced by persuading more people to work from home via electronic communications, trying to encourage them to go back to using public transport (whether bus, tram or rail), or getting more goods traffic off the roads and back on to the railways.

Roads in towns and throughout the south-east present the most obvious problems, but the main inter-urban routes are also becoming increasingly congested, as they are in other less obvious areas. Twenty million people live within a three-hour drive of the Lake District, thanks to the completion of the M6 in 1971. On popular weekends and especially on Bank Holidays, the problem has become acute, and the southern Lakes has become totally full of cars on a number of occasions – in 1989 the Police twice closed the area to incoming traffic. Here there are strong objections to building more or wider roads, and thus the only solution appears to be to control the demand. An entry fee has been suggested, as has making visitors leave their cars outside the Park and travel in by bus. Others hope that the prospect of congestion will keep visitors away, but this hardly helps the local residents. The problem is neatly summed up in two of the aims of the National Park which are in conflict with each other: to provide access, and to preserve the landscape. It is extremely difficult to promote such an area and encourage people to visit it without destroying something of what the

120 *A motorbike rider on the second Standedge turnpike which now runs across National Trust land.*

visitors have come to enjoy. At worst the Lake District may have to be redesignated as a National Car Park!

For most of the twentieth century there was no overall coherent national transport strategy, and the strategy for roads was often short-sighted. The gut reaction was simply to give more money for road building when problems became serious, partly prompted by the need to keep car-owning voters happy. But there has also been a very strong 'roads lobby' at Westminster, which seemed to include The Department of Transport, often cynically referred to as The Department of Roads. Most of the solutions adopted were belated, piecemeal, inadequate and driven by public opinion; they frequently did little more than shift the congestion further down the road. Such a reactive strategy ignored most of the fundamental issues.

In 1998 the then newly amalgamated Department of Environment, Transport and the Regions issued a number of papers about an integrated transport policy, involving drastic cuts in the road building programme, and encouraging people to travel by public transport instead of by car. The latest plan makes little mention of new road building; in the ten years to 2010 the main reference to road improvement is to 'widening 360 miles of trunk roads' as one way of tackling congestion *(Transport 2010)*. It remains to be seen whether this strategy will work.

Nevertheless it is clear that, whatever happens in future transport planning, roads will remain as the main element of the transport system of Britain, for as Scott-Giles said in 1946:

so long as men travel by land the road will go on.

BIBLIOGRAPHY

[Other editions, reprints and revisions are indicated in square brackets]

Aitken, R. (1980) *The West Highland Way* [1984, 1990]

Albert, W. (1972) *The Turnpike Road System in England, 1663-1840*

Aldcroft, D. H. (1975) *British Transport since 1914*

Allen, M. (1994) *The Roman Route across the Northern Lake District*

Allison, K. J. (1976) *The East Riding of Yorkshire Landscape*

Anderson, R. M. C. (1932) *The Roads of England*

Bagshawe, R. W. (1979) *Roman Roads* [1994]

Barnes, B. (1981) *Passage Through Time*

Belloc, H. (1910) *The Old Road* [1904]

Belloc, H. (1913) *The Stane Street*

Belloc, H. (1923) *The Road* [1924]

Bettey, J. H. (1986) *Wessex from AD 1000*

Bonser, K. J. (1970) *The Drovers*

Cochrane, C. (1969) *The Lost Roads of Wessex* [1972]

Colyer, R. (1976) *The Welsh Cattle Drovers*

Colyer, R. (1984) *Roads and Trackways of Wales*

Copeland, J. (1968) *Roads and their Traffic, 1750-1850*

Cossons, A. (1934) *The Turnpike Roads of Nottinghamshire*

Crofts, J. (1967) *Packhorse, Waggon and Post. Land Carriage and Communications under the Tudors and Stuarts*

Crosby, A (1999) *Leading the Way; a History of Lancashire's Roads*

Crosher, G. R. (1973) *Along the Chiltern Ways*

Curtis, N. (1999) *The Ridgeway* (National Trail Guide)

Dodd, A. E. and E. M. (1980) *Peakland Roads and Trackways*

Drake, J. (1969) *Motorways*

Dunn, M. (1986) *Walking Ancient Trackways*

Dyos, H. J. and Aldcroft, D. H. (1969) *British Transport – An Economic Survey from the Seventeenth Century to the Twentieth* [1974]

Fenton, A. and Stell, G. (1984) *Loads and Roads in Scotland and Beyond*

Fiennes, C. (1982) *The Illustrated Journeys of Celia Fiennes* (ed. C. Morris) [1995]

Fuller, G. J. (1953) 'The development of roads in the Surrey-Sussex Weald and coastlands between 1700 and 1900' *Institute of British Geographers: Transactions & Papers* 19

Godwin, F. and Toulson, S. (1977) *The Drovers' Roads of Wales* [1987, 1992]

Graystone, P. (1992) *Walking Roman Roads in Bowland*

Graystone, P. (1996) *Walking Roman Roads in the Fylde and Ribble Valley*

Gregory, J. W. (1931) *The Story of the Road* [1938]

Groves, R. (1972) 'Roads and Tracks' in Gill, C., *Dartmoor – A New Study*

Haldane, A. R. B. (1962) *New Ways Through the Glens* [1973, 1995]

Haldane, A. R. B. (1973) *The Drove Roads of Scotland* [1995]

Hannigan, D. (1994) *Ancient Tracks; Walking through Historic Britain*

Hemery, E. (1986) *Walking Dartmoor's Ancient Tracks* [1991]

Herbstein, D. (1982) *The North Downs Way*

Hey, D. (1980) *Packmen, Carriers and Packhorse Roads*

Hindle, B. P. (1990) *Medieval Town Plans* [2002]

Hindle, B. P. (1993) *Roads, Tracks, and their Interpretation*

Hindle, B. P. (1998a) *Roads and Tracks of the Lake District* [1984]

Hindle, B. P. (1998b) *Maps for Local Historians* [1988]

Hindle, B. P. (1998c) *Medieval Roads and Tracks* [1982, 1989]

Hindley, G. (1971) *A History of Roads*

Hollowell, S. (2000) *Enclosure Records for Historians*

Hooke, D. (1977) 'The Reconstruction of Ancient Routeways' *The Local Historian* 12

Hoskins, W. G. (1955) *The Making of the English Landscape* [1970, 1977, 1988]

Jackman, W. T. (1916) *The Development of Transportation in Modern England* [1962, 1966]

Jennett, S. (1971) *The Pilgrims' Way*

Jennett, S. (1976) *The Ridgeway Path*

Johnston, D. E. (1979) *Roman Roads in Britain*

Jones, B. and Mattingly, D. (1990) *An Atlas of Roman Britain*

Jusserand, J. J. (1889) *English Wayfaring Life in the Middle Ages* [1920, 1950, 1961]

Kain, R.J.P. and Prince, H.C. (2000) *Tithe Surveys for Historians*

Kerr, J. (1991) *Highland Highways: Old Roads in Atholl*

Livingstone, H. (1995) *In the Footsteps of Cæsar; Walking Roman Roads in Britain*

Long Distance Walker's Handbook (6th ed.) (1998)

Margary, I. D. (1948) *Roman Ways in the Weald* [1965]

Margary, I. D. (1973) *Roman Roads in Britain* [1955]

Maxwell, I. S. (1976) *Historical Atlas of West Penwith*

Moir, D. G. (1975) *Scottish Hill Tracks – Old Highways and Drove Roads* [1995, 1999]

Munby, L. M. (1977) *The Hertfordshire Landscape*

Pawson, E. (1977) *Transport and Economy – the Turnpike Roads of Eighteenth-Century Britain*

Pearce, R. M. (1978) *Thomas Telford*

Peel, J. H. B. (1976) *Along the Green Roads of Britain* [1982]

Porter, J. (1980) *The Making of the Central Pennines*

Raistrick, A. (1978) *Green Roads in the Mid-Pennines*

Ramblers' Association: www.ramblers.org.uk

Richardson, A. and Allan, T. M. (1990) 'The Roman road over the Kirkstone Pass: Ambleside to Old Penrith' *Transactions of the Cumberland & Westmorland Antiquarian & Archaeological Society* 90

Riddall, J & Trevelyan J. (1992) *Rights of Way; a Guide to Law and Practice*

Robertson, A. E. (1947) 'Old Tracks, Cross-country Routes and 'Coffin Roads' in the North-west Highlands' (*Scottish Mountaineering Club Journal*)

Robinson, B. (1986) *The Peddars Way and Norfolk Coast Path* [1992, 1996]

Russell, E. and R. C. (1982) *Landscape Changes in South Humberside*

Russell, E. and R. C. (1983) *Making New Landscapes in Lincolnshire*

Russell, E. and R. C. (1985) *Old and New Landscapes in the Horncastle Area*

Russell, E. and R. C. (1987) *Parliamentary Enclosure and New Lincolnshire Landscapes*

Scott-Giles, C. W. (1946) *The Road Goes On*

Sheldon, G. (1928) *From Trackway to Turnpike, An illustration from East Devon*

Silver, O. (1987) *The Roads of Fife*

Steane, J. (1974) *The Northamptonshire Landscape*

Stephens, W. B. (1981) *Sources for English Local History* [1973, 1975, 1994]

Stephenson, T. (1969) *The Pennine Way*

Storer, R. (1991) *Exploring Scottish Hill Tracks*

Strong, L. A. G. (1956) *The Rolling Road*

Sugden, K. (1991) *Walking the Pilgrim Ways*

Taylor, C. (1979) *Roads and Tracks of Britain* [1994]

Taylor, W. (1976) *The Military Roads in Scotland* [1996]

Thomas, J. M. (1970) *Roads before the Railways, 1700-1851*

Timperley, H. W. and Brill, E. (1983) *Ancient Trackways in Wessex* [1965]

Toulson, S. (1983) *The Moors of the Southwest; 1 Exploring the Ancient Tracks of Sedgemoor and Exmoor*

Toulson, S. (1984) *The Moors of the Southwest; 2 Exploring the Ancient Tracks of Dartmoor, Bodmin and Penwith*

Toulson, S. (1980) *The Drovers*

Transport 2010: The 10 Year Plan (2000) (Department of the Environment, Transport and the Regions: www.detr.gov.uk)

Turner, M. (1980) *English Parliamentary Enclosure*

Viatores, The (1964) *Roman Roads in the South-East Midlands*

Watkins, A. (1925) *The Old Straight Track* [1974]

Webb, S. and B. (1913) *English Local Government. Vol. 5. The Story of the King's Highway*

Wilkinson, T.W. (1900) *The Highways and Byways of England*

Williams, L. A. (1975) *Road Transport in Cumbria in the Nineteenth Century*

Wright, G. N. (1985) *Roads and Trackways of the Yorkshire Dales*

Wright, G. N. (1988) *Roads and Trackways of Wessex*

Wright, G. N. (1992) *Turnpike Roads*

Yelling, J. A. (1977) *Common Field and Enclosure in England*

INDEX